Financial Statement Basics

From Confusion to Comfort in Under 100 Pages

By Axel Tracy

Copyright © 2015 Bidi Capital Pty Ltd.
All rights reserved.

Disclaimer

The material in this publication (the "book") and the information accessed through it is of a general nature only and does not contain investment recommendations or professional advice. The information is not to be relied upon as being accurate, complete or up to date. Axel Tracy (the "author") recommends that, before acting or not acting upon information contained or referred to in this book, readers should seek independent professional advice that takes into account their financial situation, investment objectives, particular needs and/or other personal circumstances. The information contained in this book is not to be used for any purpose other than educational purposes and it is not to be construed as an indication or prediction of future results from any investment. Axel Tracy does not offer financial, business or academic advice. To the maximum extent permitted by law, the author and publisher disclaim all responsibility and liability to any person, arising from directly or indirectly from any person taking or not taking action based upon the information in this publication.

For Matt: *Your development skills and open communication changed my life in 2011, a big thanks to you.*

For The MDC Teaching Team: *Thanks for opening up the 'other side' of accounting
…I'm working hard on my balanced scorecard!*

Table of Contents

About the Author 8
About accofina.com 9
Preface 10

Book 1: Balance Sheet Basics 12
Introduction 13
Example Balance Sheet 16
What the Balance Sheet Shows...in under 2 Pages 20
The Balance Sheet Equality 24
Current & Non-Current Definitions 26
Assets 27
   Current Assets 29
   Non-Current Assets 31
Liabilities 39
   Current Liabilities 41
   Non-Current Liabilities 44
Equity 48
Links between the Balance Sheet and the Income Statement
(the Profit & Loss Statement) 52
Conclusion 54

Book 2: Income Statement Basics 56
Introduction 57
Example Income Statement 60
Housekeeping 63
   Income Statement Formatting 63
   Income Statement naming conventions 63
   Brackets within financial statements and other accounting
   documents 64
Quick Guide to the Income Statement 66
   Explaining the Income Statement in a Few Paragraphs 66
   Accrual Accounting: A Vital Concept in Income Statement
   Analysis 68

The Income Statement linking into Other Financial Statements 69
Income 71
Expenses 75
    Operating Expenses 81
Income from Operations 84
Non-operating income and expenses 85
Income Before Taxes 87
    Provision for Income Taxes 88
Equity-method investment activity 90
Net income (loss) 93
Earnings per Share Data 97
Quick Summary & Lead into Comprehensive Income Statement 101
Other Comprehensive Income (OCI) 102
Conclusion 112

Book 3: Cash Flow Statement Basics 114

Introduction 115
    Naming Conventions 117
    Formatting 117
What's Different from Previous Titles in this Series? 119
    Increased use of Sub-Headings and Sub-Sections 119
    Working from Example Statement Bottom-to-Top and not Top-to-Bottom 119
    Section Structures Repeat Throughout 120
    More Analysis Sections and Less Accounting Theory 121
The Cash Flow Statement in a Few Paragraphs 122
    Cash Flow from Financing Activities 122
    Cash Flow from Investing Activities 123
    Cash Flow from Operating Activities 123
    Cash Flow Equation 124
Example Cash Flow Statements 125
    Why we are using Two Examples 125
    Similarities & Differences between the Two Examples 126
    Source of Examples 128

The Cash Flow Statements 130
Cash (Flow Statement) is King: The benefits of the cash flow statement 134
    You Spend Cash, not Profits 135
    Cash & Different Accounting Methods 136
    Cash & Valuation 137
    Cash & Business Success 137
Cash Flows from Financing Activities 139
    Examples of Cash Flows Arising in This Section 139
    How This Section Feeds into the Cash Flow Equation 139
    What Does This Section Describe 140
    What Could the Results Be Telling Us About the Business 141
Cash Flows from Investing Activities 147
    Examples of Cash Flows Arising in This Section 147
    How This Section Feeds into the Cash Flow Equation 148
    What Does This Section Describe 149
    What Could the Results Be Telling Us About the Business 150
Cash Flows from Operating Activities 157
    Why This Section Has Been Left Till Last 157
    Examples of Cash Flows Arising in This Section 160
    How This Section Feeds into the Cash Flow Equation 162
    What Does This Section Describe 162
    What Could the Results Be Telling Us About the Business 164
Specific Accounting Issues that may be presented in Cash Flow Statements 173
    FX Translation Issues 173
    Significant Non-Cash Disclosures 176
    Interest & Dividends 178
    Taxes 180
Final Thoughts 182

Extras 184
Book Excerpt 184
Free (and One Paid) Accounting Resources 190
Free accofina.com Resources 193
More Books and Other accofina Products 195

accofina Contact Details and Review Request.........................197

About the Author

Axel Tracy is an accounting and business student at the University of Technology, Sydney (UTS) and is a new financial planning student at the Northern Sydney Institute. He has a passion for his studies and is a member of the invitation-only Golden Key International Honours Society in recognition of having a GPA that placed him in the top bracket of students at his university. He is also a member of the UTS Honour Society.

He was employed by the University of Technology, Sydney, to run PASS sessions in the subject of Accounting Standards and Regulations, an undergraduate accounting subject that trains students to become familiar with Australia's implementation of International Financial Reporting Standards, the current Australian accounting standards regime. He was also employed by UTS as a one-on-one tutor for the study of another 2nd year accounting subject, Accounting for Business Combinations, a subject that dealt with the financial accounting of corporate groups, joint ventures and associates.

Since April, 2011, he has been the Founder & Manager of RatioAnalysis.net, a website dedicated to financial and accounting ratios.

In August, 2013, Axel launched accofina.com. This website promotes the sale of products involved with accounting and finance knowledge and education.

Axel lives in Armidale, Australia, and apart from studies or working on accofina, enjoys spending time with his partner, Sarah, relishing a good cup of coffee or indulging in too much CNBC.

Axel's 'Amazon Author' Page:
http://www.amazon.com/author/axeltracy

About accofina.com

accofina.com launched in August, 2013, and is a hub for accounting & finance knowledge and technology.

On the website you will find Books (Free & Paid), iOS Apple Apps, Online Courses & Tutorials, Free MS Excel Spreadsheets and other Free Online Calculators all customized to assist putting academic accounting & finance knowledge, through technology, in the hands of businesspeople, investors and students.

accofina.com is part of Bidi Capital Pty Ltd, which is a company founded, directed and owned by this book's author, Axel Tracy.

Preface

Welcome to this bundled book series that I am very proud to present! This title, which is actually three smaller books combined into one, is the culmination of a number of years in my early 30s. The first of the three books I wrote (Balance Sheet Basics) was written in 2013, the second (Income Statement Basics) came around in 2014 and the final title (Cash Flow Statement Basics) was one that I just finished and released in the final days of 2015.

What does this all mean to you? (1) Hopefully my skills as an author and product developer have improved throughout the series, and this should hopefully benefit you the reader (2) In the process of developing this bundled book, I now have the time and dedicated focus to enhance any of the earlier individually released titles within an editing process.

This book is primarily about learning how to read, navigate, understand and analyse financial statements. But where the strength of this series may lie is that it not only covers financial statements but it will also give you a strong foundation in general accounting knowledge.

This book hopes to combine my accounting study and filter this knowledge through the tight lens of the financial statements. That is, you will be learning fundamental accounting and analysis skills (indirectly) through learning about the overarching financial statements (the direct lessons).

This approach may be very useful for the non-accounting trained businessperson or investor. As aside from taxation issues, which is almost a compliance matter, the financial statements will be the main interaction with your financial accounting system or be your primary available investment information. Thus, the lessons being structured in this manner may just be very practical (and useful) to you once you finished reading the book.

Further, **my primary target markets are those who have little to no accounting training**. I really do get my kicks by teaching new skills to willing readers and therefore I have tried to make this book as user-friendly as possible, while still stretching you enough to allow you to find value from your investment of time and money.

So while all three books included are brief, please be assured that you will be covering many accounting topics and skills in one. And that this time spent in developing your accounting & finance knowledge can indeed pay off handsomely in your own financial and business pursuits.

Thanks again for your interest and best of success for your upcoming read!

Axel

Book 1: Balance Sheet Basics

Introduction

Whether you are running a business or analysing an investment, you will no doubt be provided with the financial statements of the business. These statements can be daunting if you are unsure about how to read them, yet it is imperative to have some accounting knowledge if you want to know the true state of a business. The financial statements, in short, give you a condensed glance into the financial success of any business.

While country-specific regulation dictates which financial statements must be prepared by an entity, the three key financial statements are:

1) The Income Statement (The Profit & Loss Statement)
2) The Balance Sheet (The Statement of Financial Position)
3) The Cash Flow Statement

This book will cover the basics of (2) The Balance Sheet, and will be part of a series of all three of these statements.

This book is not aimed at accountants or financial advisors, it is aimed at those who are provided with financial statements yet do not have an accounting background. Warren Buffett has said that accounting is the "language of business" so this book should hopefully teach you a few key 'phrases' that will allow you to converse about, and navigate around, the balance sheet. Will you become an expert from this book alone? No, but the beauty of the key financial statements is that a basic level of knowledge will allow you to make leaps and bounds when it comes to extracting value from the statements; in this case, the balance sheet.

Hopefully you should be able to tear through this read in one or two sittings, and you'll be prepped to make better business and investment decisions the next time someone hands you a balance sheet.

The structure of this book is pretty straightforward. Important concepts behind the balance sheet are covered along with outlines and descriptions of its components. Immediately after this introduction you will find an example balance sheet, and you can refer to this example as you progress through the chapters.

I am educated in accounting…and not educated in writing! I write because I like to help people learn accounting concepts…and I am passionate about accounting! I mention this because while I'd love to be a best-selling author, I know I will never become a best-writing author. The best I can hope for is that I become a better writer through each book being published over time. You can help me achieve these two goals:

If you want to help me become a better writer, please email me at **axel@accofina.com** and give me your suggestions for improvement.

If you want to help me become a best-selling author, please leave a positive review for this book (and maybe a comment on how it helped you) on Amazon.com.

So let's get into it!

Take a look at the Balance Sheet on the next page, look at its components and headings and then dive into the rest of this eBook. Best wishes!

Example Balance Sheet

Amazon.com Inc. (NASDAQ: AMZN)
Balance Sheet for 31st December, 2012

Extracted from Google Finance (**https://www.google.com/finance**), a great free site for company analysis.

(In Millions of USD)

Assets

Current Assets

Cash & Equivalents	$8,084
Short-Term Investments	$3,364
Accounts Receivable – Net	$3,364
Inventory	$6,031
Prepaid Expenses	$0
Other Current Assets	$453
Total Current Assets	**$21,296**

Non-Current Assets

Property, Plant & Equipment (PPE) – Cost	$9,582
Accumulated Depreciation (PPE)	($2,522)
Goodwill – Net	$2,552
Intangibles	$725
Long Term Investments	$0
Other Non-Current Assets	$922
Total Non-Current Assets	**$11,259**

Total Assets

$32,555

Liabilities

Current Liabilities
Accounts Payable	$13,318
Accrued Expenses	$5,684
Notes Payable/Short Term Debt	$0
Current portion of Long Term Debt/Capital Leases	$0
Other Current Liabilities	$0
Total Current Liabilities	**$19,002**

Non-Current Liabilities
Long Term Debt	$3,084
Capital/Finance Lease Obligations	$746
Deferred Income Tax Liabilities	$0
Other Liabilities	$1,531
Total Non-Current Liabilities	**$5,361**

Total Liabilities $24,363

Equity

Common Stock – Total	$5
Additional Paid in Capital	$8,347
Retained Earnings	$1,916
Treasury Stock – Common	($1837)
Other Equity	($239)

Total Equity $8,192

Total Liabilities & Equity
$32,555

Note: While I tried to make this balance sheet as practical as possible, there is no global standard on how you set out a balance sheet. Sure, assets, liabilities & equity are always there, but different countries include different specifics. This may include account names (the balance sheet line items) and of course currencies.

What's more is that as the size and complexity of a business grows, so does the complexity of the balance sheet. This book is published as part of a small business, and if you looked at my company's balance sheet you would see it is far simpler and has less accounts than a behemoth like Amazon Inc. So, if you have a balance sheet for your business and things don't match up exactly to what's above or what's on Google Finance, then don't stress, just keep in mind that the following sections should appear in all balance sheets:

- Assets
    - Current Assets
    - Non-Current Assets
- Liabilities
    - Current Liabilities
    - Non-Current Liabilities
- Equity
    - Capital
    - Retained Earnings
    - Current Earnings (if the balance sheet is prepared during the financial year)

Also, just before we jump ahead, take a look at the equality between assets and then liabilities plus equity: these MUST always balance. Assets must be equal to the sum of liabilities and equity. This is just part of double-entry accounting (a topic outside the scope of this book). But another way to look at it is: your assets must always be financed by debt (liabilities) and/or equity. In other words, you can't pay for something in the business unless you get the money from somewhere, such as a bank, investors or the business earnings (current and retained earnings).

Finally, I have tried to take what's on Google Finance and reproduce it above for the novice reader. So if you take a look online yourself, you will see it's not an exact replica. Again, don't stress, get a hold of the basics and you will eventually be able to analyse any balance sheet out there. If you do want to look at the Google Finance balance sheet, follow these steps:

1) Go to **www.google.com/finance**
2) In the "Search Finance" box, type: Amazon.com and choose Amazon.com, Inc. from the search drop-down
3) Under the Company Menu (left-hand side) choose "Financials"
4) Click Balance Sheet
5) Click Annual Data
6) You will now find the above balance sheet where "As of 2012-12-31" lies.

What the Balance Sheet Shows…in under 2 Pages

So why do we have a balance sheet in the first place? Why are you reading this book?

Here's the super-short answer:

A balance sheet shows (denominated in currency) what a business:

1) Owns/Controls (Assets)
2) Owes/Obligated to do (Liabilities)
3) And what's left when you subtracted [2] from [1]: What is left for the owners' of the business (Equity)

That's really all there is to it!

If you wanted to produce a balance sheet for a company like Amazon.com then that would take years of study and practice, and many others (just as skilled as you) to help you…but you can't hide the fact that the end result of any balance sheet is just in the numbered list above.

So what use is this information?

Well, the first word of caution is that while the Balance Sheet is vital for company analysis, it is not a stand-alone statement. You generally need to look at the other financial statements (e.g. Income Statement and Statement of Cash Flows) to get the true picture of what is going on behind the numbers.

But leaving that word of caution aside, there is still lots you can understand from a balance sheet.

First, look at the assets (what the company owns). Assets have a complicated definition in the financial accounting handbook but essentially assets are what generate future income of the business. A company purchases, or holds, assets in the hope that they will produce more income than they cost to buy or hold. Simple. Look at "Inventory" (Current Assets) in the example Balance Sheet; this account represents goods that Amazon.com has purchased in the hope that it can later re-sell them at a higher price. Or "Property, Plant & Equipment" (Non-Current Assets), this account represents the property, plant & equipment (go figure!) that Amazon.com has purchased that will hopefully help their business run smoothly (such as a warehouse and logistics machinery), which will in turn hopefully lead it to sell more books like this one.

Next, look at the liabilities (what the company owes). Again, there is a complicated definition for liabilities in the handbook, but generally what it refers to are the obligations that lead to outflows of currency at later date(s) to satisfy these same obligations. In short, you can think of them as simply the debts of the business.

These debts can represent how you funded the assets on the other side of the balance sheet (note: you can also fund them through equity). For instance, you took on a bank loan of $100,000 (a liability) to purchase a retail shop for a business (an asset in the property, plant and equipment line item). And then this asset will hopefully lead to income in the future.

The final section is equity. Now I have talked about the financial accounting handbook definitions of the previous two components, but the definition of equity is rather abstract in that is based on a derivative of the previous two definitions (of assets & liabilities). The better way to look at equity is to think of it as what is left for the owners of the business if all the assets were liquidated and the liabilities paid off. Equity represents owner, or shareholder, funds that have been invested, or retained, in the business (although this is not the exact definition).

Similar to liabilities, equity can also be a source of funds to pay for assets. So rather than take out that bank loan to buy the retail shop, the business could sell stock/shares in the business for $100,000 and then buy the shop, or simply use the funds it has earned in business operations (as these 'Retained Earnings' are also equity).

Let's put it all together in a timeline:

    (1) A business is incorporated and starts its life

    (2) It raises money through taking on liabilities or issuing equity

    (3) It uses this money to buy assets

    (4) The assets generate income

    (5) The income can pay for more assets or the cycle repeats from stage (2)

But outside of this timeline, never forget than any balance sheet simply shows a snapshot in time of what a business:

- "Owns" (assets)
- "Owes" (liabilities)
- "What is left for the owners of the business" (equity)

If you can remember this then you can start to paint a picture of the business.

For instance, you can tell how the management likes to finance the business (does it have higher liabilities or higher equity), you can look at line items and see how the assets are structured (e.g. does it have lots of cash or lots of fixed, non-current assets), whether the business is over-leveraged (are liabilities too high in relation to assets), etc.

These are just a few examples, just think about what the components of the balance sheet represent, spend time analyzing the overall figures and relationships and start to paint that picture of what is going on underneath all those raw numbers.

The Balance Sheet Equality

I mentioned this briefly in the Example Amazon Balance Sheet Section, and also mentioned double-entry accounting. While not explaining double-entry accounting in full, I do want to talk about the Balance Sheet Equality.

The balance sheet equality is based on the "Accounting Equation".

Simply, the accounting equation is a rule that must hold. If it does not hold then that is an immediate signal that you have made a mistake in your accounting processes, your double-entry accounting.

Here is the equation:

Assets = Liabilities + Equity

Like I mentioned earlier, to finance an asset you must source those funds from liabilities or equity (or both). For example, when assets go up by, say, $10,000 then either you have taken on a liability and/or issued equity for the same amount of $10,000, and the accounting equation will hold. None of the components, assets, liabilities or equity can simply 'appear' (or disappear) without another component (or the same component, but a different account line item) being affected.

Try it out for yourself…have a look at Amazon's Balance Sheet and see if any of the items (or 'accounts' as they're properly called) could just 'appear'. When you realize they couldn't, try and see which corresponding account(s) could be affected by a change in the initial account you are looking at. For example, where did Cash & Cash Equivalents come from? It could be a loan (liability), from current earnings (equity), from issuing stock/shares (equity again) or maybe even from selling some property, plant and equipment or inventory (assets themselves), etc.

The accounting equation is at the heart of 'double-entry accounting'. This is the idea that not only does every transaction affect an account of assets, liabilities or equity, but also every transaction affects *at least two accounts* (hence double-entry) within these components. Without going into a lesson about 'debits' and 'credits' (the core theory behind recording transactions in the double-entry system), the fact that each transaction affects at least two accounts means that the accounting equation MUST always balance. It's not that YOU must make it balance, it's simply that if it doesn't balance then there has been a clerical error in recording a transaction within a double-entry system. For example, remember that $100,000 loan to buy the retail shop? Well, that would be Liabilities increasing by $100,000 (the loan) and Assets increasing by $100,000 (the retail shop)…and the equation holds. This example can be replicated (and the accounting equation will still hold) by every single transaction any possible business is making or ever could make. It is simply that comprehensive…a pretty powerful concept behind what is too often raw, not-understood numbers on a simple, 1-page balance sheet.

Current & Non-Current Definitions

Okay, let's cover some jargon now that will bleed through the rest of this book…

In the balance sheet, both assets and liabilities are broken down into "Current" and "Non-Current". What does this mean? It is simply accountants' jargon defining time periods.

'Current' means the asset will be "realized" (used up or turned into cash) within the next 12-month period. A 'Non-Current" asset is just an asset that will be realized beyond the next 12-month period. Twelve months from the date of the balance sheet is the line in the sand, the barrier between current and non-current.

The flip side is true for liabilities. All liabilities that must be settled (paid back) within the next 12-months are considered 'Current' liabilities. Those that don't need to be settled for at least 12-months are considered 'Non-Current' liabilities.

Assets

"An asset is a resource controlled by the entity as a result of past events, and from which future economic benefits are expected to flow to the entity"

- IASB Conceptual Framework: Chapter 4 The Framework; paragraph 4.4(a)

The definition above is the 'complicated' definition of an asset, which I mentioned earlier. The definition comes from the International Accounting Standards Board (IASB), a financial accounting standards (rules) organization that sets the standards for all nations who follow international accounting standards.

Breaking the jargon down, the definition is not too complicated. An asset is something that is "controlled" by a business (like a factory) due to a "past" transaction (buying the factory), which causes a flow to the business of "future economic benefits", i.e. income will be derived from using the asset in the future (the factory will produce goods in the future that will be sold for income).

Technically, anything that fits inside the above definition could be called an asset. And these are what sit at the top of the balance sheet.

The key idea is that an asset is acquired and/or held by a business in order to generate, or access, cash from it in the future.

Generally, the convention is that assets are listed in order of liquidity down the balance sheet. That means that the most liquid assets (e.g. cash) sit at the top of the list of assets and the least liquid (perhaps an oil transport tanker) sit at the bottom. The term "liquidity" simply refers to the ability to turn the asset into cash. If the asset is considered highly liquid, then it is easy to convert into cash, if it considered highly illiquid, then it is hard to convert into cash.

Taking on board these key ideas, have a look at the Amazon Inc. balance sheet. What can you deduce from the assets listed in this financial statement? Are the highest asset values located near the top, implying lots of liquid assets? What does each asset value tell you about the Amazon business model, e.g. does it use high levels of equipment fixed assets, or possibly have high levels of accounts receivable?

I cannot stress enough the concept of asking yourself, when you look at the balance sheet, "what does this tell me?" If you spend enough time analyzing the accounts, you can start to draw inferences about the business. For example, I just mentioned testing whether the accounts receivable is high, you could spend time comparing the accounts receivable balance over time (over multiple balance sheets) and test if this asset figure is rising or falling. A fall may mean that the business is improving its collections operations, or maybe that it is tightening its credit policy. When you draw one conclusion, you can often check its validity by looking at other sections of the financial statements. For example, if the business was tightening its credit policy, what has happened to sales revenue in the Income Statement? One could assume that a very tight credit policy might mean fewer sales as fewer clients would qualify for credit.

While this last paragraph is more about financial statement analysis rather than understanding balance sheets, I hope you can appreciate the idea that while this concise book can help you get your head around a balance sheet you can always learn more and get more value from all financial statements.

Current Assets

Now that we've covered the definitions of 'current' and 'assets' we can take a little more time looking at specific current assets.

Remembering that the current assets are the most liquid since they are at the top of the balance sheet, you will soon realize that many current assets are, in fact, monetary in nature. That is, they are a claim to some sort of finances. Where the Property, Plant & Equipment (a non-current asset) value represents something like a factory in a city, many of the current assets specifically represent financial claims (like 'Cash' or 'Accounts Receivable').

Let's add a quick finance concept before moving onto analyzing current assets…

We mentioned that asset liquidity refers to assets ability to be converted to cash. You may ask why a business would give up liquid assets (which can pay the invoices that come in or pay dividends to owners) for less liquid assets (which may involve a lengthy process before using them to pay the invoices or dividends)? The answer lies in the general principle that a business (or even an individual) gives up liquidity in order to (hopefully) obtain a higher return from the asset. Look at Amazon Inc's top two current assets, 'Cash & Equivalents' and 'Short-Term Investments': now both are highly liquid (they both sit right at the top), but from their order you can see that cash is more liquid than short-term investments. Now that makes sense, you can simply go to your bank and make a withdrawal from Cash today, yet you may need a few days or few weeks to sell the Short-Term Investments and wait for the delayed settlement to realize their cash value. But look what also makes sense: do you expect a higher return from your checking account interest rate (Cash & Equivalents) or from your corporate bonds (Short-Term Investments)? While not only fitting into the 'Current Assets' section alone, this lesson is important to remember for the rest of this book and your own balance sheet analysis.

Now with this lesson under our belt, what can we learn from the current assets section of a balance sheet? One, of many, things we can draw is that we can test how 'secure' the business will be at maintaining its operations. As mentioned, you can generally only pay the business' bills with cash, and you only really ever go out of business if you can't pay your bills. So knowing this we can look at the structure of a business' current assets. If 'Inventory' is too high, it may mean that the entity can't sell is stock or maintain optimal stock levels in-store. If 'Accounts Receivable' is too high then it may mean that the entity can't collect its debts adequately. Yet, if the more liquid current assets are too high, then this may mean that the entity is forsaking a higher return on its assets for the sake of having lots of cash and short-term investments.

Knowing what to look for, and how to interpret values, will take practice, but even within these past few pages you can begin to start telling the story of the business from what may have been an almost 'foreign' set of line items and values.

Non-Current Assets

Next we are looking at non-current assets; these being the assets that are expected to last, or remain on the balance sheet (individually) for more than 12-months.

We spend quite a bit of time on non-current assets in comparison to other sections. The reason for this is two-fold.

First, there are some new accounting concepts and terminology introduced into this section of the balance sheet. It makes non-current assets not as quickly understandable as some of the other sections of the statement. Therefore we go into a few specific accounts inside non-current assets and try to explain the accounting and jargon behind them.

Secondly, more likely than not, the non-current assets are vital to the operation and success of the business. This is because very often the revenue-generation capabilities of a business are based on its ability to turn non-current assets into sales. Investments in non-current assets are what lead to future sales. As you read the sections below try imagining any business without an efficient set of non-current assets, generally there would be no business at all. All accounts of the balance sheet play their part and have a role in managing a business, but it is success (or lack of it) of investments in non-current assets that lead to the income-production success of a business. Refer back to the Current Asset section and our discussion on liquidity. We said that liquidity is often given up for a higher return on the assets. This implies the least liquid assets (the non-current assets) can earn the highest returns and may lead to the highest success for the business. Truly understanding this section of the balance sheet, and spending more time on it, leads to a better understanding of the revenue-generation profile of any business.

Firstly, let's look at Amazon's non-current assets. While a couple of accounts, i.e. Property, Plant & Equipment (PPE) and Long Term Investments are things we have already covered or are otherwise self explanatory, there are a few accounts in our example balance sheet that you will see in many other businesses and deserve special attention. These are Accumulated Depreciation, Intangibles & Goodwill.

Accumulated Depreciation:

When a non-current asset is purchased, such as an item of PPE, the cost of the asset goes straight on the balance sheet without appearing in the corresponding Profit & Loss Statement in the Expenses section. This is just a rule of accounting, but does this mean that a hypothetical $50,000 Forklift never appears as an expense for the business? The answer is 'No' and the 'Depreciation Expense' account gives the explanation. Without going too deep into some of the fundamental principles of accounting, specifically the 'matching principle', try to look at it like this:

If Amazon buys a $50,000 forklift in January, 2014, and that forklift is expected to carry orders from warehouse shelves to delivery trucks for *two full years*, then which Profit and Loss Statement structure would look more accurate (1) A full $50,000 PPE Expense in the January 2014 Profit and Loss Statement and therefore $0 PPE Expense for every profit and loss statement from there, or (2) considering the forklift will help generate revenue for *two full years* (and hence is an asset), we should have 24 separate monthly profit and loss statements (if we report monthly) and recognize a portion of the $50,000 as an expense in each of the separate 24 statements, i.e. $2,083.33 PPE Expense for each month over 24-months ($50,000/24 = $2,083.33). The answer is (2) because as accountants we better reflect the true state of the business if we 'match' the expenses against the revenue they generate, i.e. we 'match' the $50,000 Forklift expense against the 24-months of revenue it helps generate by delivering the orders for *two full years*.

If you are still with me at this point, then great, because you now probably understand the most common misconception that faces university accounting students. Now let's complete the circle:

In the example we just explained in the above paragraph, we actually don't recognize a $2,083.33 PPE Expense in each of the 24 monthly profit and loss statements. Instead we use a 'catch-all' account called Depreciation, so in each of those 24 statements we would have a $2,083.33 'Depreciation' Expense.

Okay, we're almost there. So, I have been talking a lot about depreciation 'expenses' and profit and loss statements…yet this is a book about balance sheets! Well, this is an example of where the two statements link. Because when every profit and loss statement is prepared and there is a depreciation expense, then this depreciation expense amount (an exact dollar figure) is transferred to the balance sheet and added to a running total of all depreciation to date for each separate depreciable non-current asset account. This running total is known as 'Accumulated Depreciation' and is known as a 'contra asset' account, meaning that the balance is negative and is subtracted from the particular non-current asset account on the balance sheet.

Taking all this on board, let's return to our forklift example: Let's imagine it is now April, 2014, and we are looking at our March balance sheet and we have already completed January, February & March profit and loss statements. Our March balance sheet would have something like this:

Non-Current Assets
PPE $50,000
(The original cost of the forklift)
Accumulated Depreciation – PPE   ($6,250)
(A negative balance that is the sum of $2,083.33 depreciation expenses in each of January, February & March)
Total Non-Current Assets $43,750
(Cost minus Depreciation or $50,000 minus $6,250)

With all of this wrapped up, hopefully you now know the concept of an Accumulated Depreciation account and why it has a negative balance. There is a little more to depreciation that what has been explained, but the key ideas outlined will always hold.

The next 'tricky' account is Intangibles.

Intangibles:

Now, I just said this account was 'tricky', but if you can get around some accounting jargon then you should understand this account with knowledge we have already covered.

The International Accounting Standards Board (the 'rule' makers of the financial accounting profession) defines an Intangible as "an identifiable non-monetary asset without physical substance"…let's break this down:

First, it's an asset. Simple.

Next, it's an asset without physical substance. This is kind of like saying you can't 'touch' it. This includes things like legal rights (e.g. patents) and computer code (e.g. software). This is opposed to an asset with physical substance, like a crane or a truck.

It's non-monetary: this simply means it is not a type of asset that represents a financial claim. Cash and Accounts Receivable are both monetary assets; their values represent a specific claim to a specific amount of cash. Therefore, all these type of monetary assets can't be classified as intangibles, even though they may meet all other criteria.

Finally, it's "identifiable". This is accounting jargon that means the asset can be separated from the business and hypothetically sold individually. Using software as an example, your business could separate your MS Office software (it wouldn't destroy your business…you simply couldn't use MS Excel, MS Word, etc.) from the rest of your business and sell the software as an individual item (if you had the hypothetical legal right to do this). These qualities of your MS Office software makes this productivity package an 'identifiable' asset.

Pull all these explanations together and we know what an Intangible Asset is. Depending on the industry, they can often be a large and vital component of a businesses asset base.

Think about software companies, how much of their value is made up of the intangible patents they own and the in-house software systems they use. The industry can also determine what type of intangibles a business has. As just explained, software companies have high levels of patents, casino companies may have high levels of gaming licenses, music companies have high levels of copyright assets, and so on.

Before we move on, do intangibles depreciate like some other non-current assets? The answer is 'sometimes' and 'not exactly'. It's 'sometimes' because some intangible have an indefinite life (and are not depreciated) and some intangibles do have a set useful life, like a patent lasting 20 years (and are depreciated). And it's 'not exactly' because intangibles don't actually depreciate, they "amortize". This is just more accounting terminology and effectively is identical to depreciation…except we have Amortization Expense and Accumulated Amortization, and not depreciation.

Goodwill:

The final account we are looking at is Goodwill.
Firstly, goodwill is a type of intangible asset but has it's own account.

Next, goodwill has two meanings, yet only one will ever apply to the balance sheet. 'Goodwill' can often refer to the positive feeling, mood or attitude towards a business: a business with great customer service has goodwill, a business with strong brand loyalty has goodwill, etc. But this type of *internally generated* goodwill is NEVER shown on the balance sheet.

The type of Goodwill in Amazon's balance sheet (and all other balance sheets) is *purchased* goodwill. What is 'purchased' goodwill? You probably know that many companies make acquisitions of other business, e.g. Google buying YouTube, Bank of America buying Merrill Lynch, etc. Purchased goodwill is a result of the accounting of these corporate transactions.

Essentially, when a business buys another business it is paying $x for the $y value of the Equity or Net Assets (value of assets minus liabilities) of the other business. Generally, to encourage the shareholders of the business being taken over to sell their stock to the acquiring company a premium must be paid. A good premium so the takeover offer seems attractive. This premium is why $x is generally higher than $y. And the difference ($z) between $x and $y is the purchased goodwill…and $z appears on the balance sheet as goodwill!

Let's use a quick example and remove the alphabet notation (note: this is a stylized example and not a representation of what really happened): Google wants to buy YouTube. YouTube has $100m of Net Assets (Assets minus Liabilities), but Google really wants the owners of YouTube to sell their stock to Google so they can take control. Therefore Google offers $1b to buy YouTube, a premium of $900m ($1b minus $100m). The Goodwill on Google's next balance sheet (post the YouTube acquisition) is $900m.

Liabilities

"A liability is a present obligation of the entity arising from past events, the settlement of which is expected to result in an outflow from the entity of resources embodying economic benefits."

- IASB Conceptual Framework: Chapter 4 The Framework; paragraph 4 4(h)

Once again the definition provided by the IASB is rather convoluted. But before we write it off, have a look at it again and then go back to the IASB definition of assets. You will see that they are almost a mirror image of each other. Rather than being a "resource controlled" it is a "present obligation" and rather than "economic benefits...flow to the entity" it is "outflow from the entity of...economic benefits". So when an asset is something you have power over that creates inflows of cash, a liabilities is something you don't have power over (it's an obligation) that creates outflows of cash.

Again like assets, there are three key components of the definition. First it is a "present obligation", not a past or future obligation it is something you owe now (like the current electricity invoice). It is based on "past events", that is you will never find a liability on a balance sheet for an event that will happen in the future (you used the electricity last month to receive the current electricity invoice) and will result in an "outflow...of resources", meaning you will settle the liability by handing over a resource (generally cash, like when you pay the electricity bill).

But still, yes, the definition is complex, detailed and a little mind-bending. If you want to strip out all the detail and jargon, a liability is a 'debt', something you owe. Technically, anything that fits the formal IASB definition of a liability should be on the balance sheet and this definition is a bit broader than simply saying 'debts'.

From here on in you will start to see the same knowledge repeating itself, just maybe with a little twist or flip. The next concept to repeat itself is the accounts being sorted based on their liquidity. When assets were listed top to bottom based on liquidity, liabilities are ordered on the balance sheet from top to bottom based on when they have to be settled. The sooner the liability has to be settled, the higher up the order it is in the liabilities section.

Once again, liabilities are broken down into current and non-current categories and also once again, even with only the knowledge covered already, we can start to paint the picture behind the numbers. Look at Amazon's liabilities, look at the current and non-current breakdown, look at which liabilities are the highest and when the have to be settled. What is this picture telling us about Amazon?

Still not grasping it 100%? Think about it like this, why does a company go out of business (if not voluntarily wound-up or acquired by another company)? Basically the answer to this question is always because it can't pay it's debts and it or its creditors put it in bankruptcy or liquidation. Wait! What's another name for debts? Liabilities. And how do we pay/settle liabilities? Cash (generally). And cash is an asset. And how do we get cash? By getting a return from our current and non-current assets.

See how it's all starting to fit together. An analysis of a company's liabilities is often an analysis of business risk. So knowing what you know now, and what was explained in this section, take another look at Amazon's balance sheet and its liabilities and try to begin to tell a story about Amazon's liabilities and possible risk. Starting to see the beauty of a 1-page balance sheet, yet?

Current Liabilities

Current liabilities on the balance sheet are those due within 12 months. This can immediately allow a quick check of the solvency status of any business. How? Simply look at the level of current liabilities and check against the level of current assets (what will pay these liabilities). Apart from a few large businesses with very high inventory turnover, this quick check is one the simplest applications of balance sheet analysis.

When you build your confidence in handling financial statements and move onto ratio analysis, this quick check of measuring current assets and current liabilities is known as the 'current ratio' and is often used to test a business' ability to maintain normal operations without resorting to selling non-current assets or raising capital. (When ready, and if interested, you can learn more about ratio analysis by reading another book of mine, *"Ratio Analysis Fundamentals: How 17 Financial Ratios Can Allow You to Analyse Any Business on the Planet"* **accofina.com/ratio-analysis-fundamentals.html**).

Apart from quick liquidity tests, the current liabilities can also give a sense of the structure of the long-term debt financing of a business. If you look at Amazon's balance sheet you'll see an account named 'Current portion of Long Term Debt/Capital Leases'. What this account represents is a transfer of long-term debt, which sits in non-current liabilities, to the current liabilities section, as this portion of this debt will be due in the coming year. Knowing this you can see how the long-term debt is structured: is the current portion remaining constant over time, meaning even and predictable payments going forward. Or is the current portion more lumpy, meaning that you will need to keep an eye on when a large 'chunk' of long term debt becomes due.

At the very top of current liabilities is Accounts Payable. This account is used for the operating expenses which are made on short term credit, for example it's kind of like that electricity invoice being sent out at the end of the month but you are given 30 days to pay it. All the operating expenses with any type of credit terms fall into accounts payable.

Again, testing near term solvency and liquidity risk is the best application of analyzing accounts payable.

Leaving the most complicated till last, Accrued Expenses represents a function of accounting practice. One of the foundations of the study of accounting is the concept of 'accrual accounting'. In short, this means we recognize transactions 'as they occur' as opposed to only 'when cash payments are made'.

Putting it in an example: if your business pays $6,000 rent on a quarterly basis (i.e. you transfer $6,000 cash to your landlord in January, April, July & October) but you prepare financial statements on a monthly basis (i.e. every month January through December), then when should you have "Rent Expense" on your Profit & Loss statement? Should it be $6,000 each in January, April, July & October? Using 'accrual accounting' (and think back to the earlier depreciation explanation) we should recognize "Rent Expense" every time we prepare financial statements, after all, we have used the rental property every day of the year and not just in January, April, etc. Therefore, since we prepare financial statements monthly (January through December) we should recognize $2,000 ($6,000 / 3) "Rent Expense" in every month January through December. But in Feb & March, and every month where we don't receive a rent bill/invoice, where do we show the amount owing from the 'accrued' rent expense? We don't hand over cash in these months so our current asset Cash doesn't go down, and we don't have a bill yet in these months so we can't put the $2,000 in Accounts Payable. The answer lies in the Accrued Expenses account (still a liability account). In February we put $2,000 in Accrued Expenses, in March we put another $2,000 there and have a balance of $4,000 and then in April (when we actually get the bill or hand over cash) we show another $2,000 rent expense in our Profit & Loss Statement but we clear Accrued Expenses back to $0 and transfer the full $6,000 to accounts payable (if we have credit terms) or take the full $6,000 from the cash account (if we paid immediately as we don't have credit terms).

Non-Current Liabilities

Next up we have non-current liabilities, and to be honest we are not going to spend as much time covering this section (in comparison to non-current assets). The reason for this is that, firstly, non-current liabilities are generally made of long-term debt and that concept should be self-explanatory, and secondly, a couple of the accounts within non-current liabilities are a little beyond the scope of this book; in fact you will find many early accounting graduates would struggle to adequately explain them to a novice who did not have formal university accounting training.

Let's cover the simple stuff:

Long-Term Debt is simply the loans that are due beyond 12-months. The dollar value given is simply what is left to be repaid, the loan principal in addition to accumulated interest. The major take-away from these figures are leverage analysis and, once again, risk analysis.

Leverage is term given to how much of a business is debt financed. It's termed leverage because it 'levers' the upside or downside. In other words, by increasing the capital base with a loan you can magnify your gains or magnify your losses depending on how successful your strategy and implementation is. So when you look at the Long-Term Debt figures, you can assess how aggressive a management is: have they been highly 'leveraging' their business, and if so, do they have the right strategy and implementation? Or is this increased debt putting the company at risk? Which leads into risk analysis. We have covered this a number of times already, but liabilities are a source of risk, so looking at Long-Term

Debt values allows us to measure the level of risk in the capital structure of the business.

The account Other Liabilities is simply a catchall for all more miscellaneous liabilities. And if we remember our formal IASB definition of liabilities, we can conclude that ANYTHING that fits that definition of liabilities has to be on the balance sheet. This can be pretty widely encompassing, so there needs to be some sort of catchall account.

Now to the stuff that requires deep training…so much so that we are going to brush over it with only a few pointers in this 'basics' book:

Firstly, the account "Capital/Finance Lease Obligations". In years past, accountants and large corporations devised an accounting 'trick' that could result in lower expenses, fewer liabilities & stronger accounting ratios and as a result improve their financial performance and borrowing capacity. This trick was to not borrow funds and then purchase large non-current assets but instead they leased them without borrowing any funds. The accounting behind this trick is too complicated for this book but when this practice became too widespread the financial accounting rule-setters like the IASB and other national equivalents (in the United States it is the FASB, the Financial Accounting Standards Board) responded by effectively outlawing this trick and forcing lease transactions that were substitutes for a 'borrow and purchase' transaction to be classified and accounted for very similarly to Long-Term Debt. In conclusion, what you need to know as a non-accountant is that the account "Capital/Finance Lease Obligations" is effectively identical to Long-Term Debt account, so you should aggregate these totals to find the true figure for non-current debts outstanding.

Finally, there is "Deferred Income Tax Liabilities". This account is there because reporting entities must use 'tax effect' accounting. Tax effect accounting as a concept is very difficult to get your head around, does not apply to all businesses, is the product of detailed and complicated (but hopefully more 'accurate') accounting theory and is often hotly-debated by accounting academics as to whether these 'liabilities' genuinely fit the definition of a liability. Thankfully, the figures for Deferred Income Tax Liabilities should be rather small and generally insignificant. For any novice, best to just acknowledge the figure and move on. For the record, there is also the possibility of having 'deferred income tax assets'.

Equity

"Equity is the residual interest in the assets of the entity after deducting all its liabilities."

- IASB Conceptual Framework: Chapter 4 The Framework; paragraph 4.4(c)

You'll see from this IASB definition that equity doesn't have its own definition but one that is a derivative based on the of both the asset and liability definitions.

The key idea about equity is that it's the owners' interest in the business. From all operations to date, equity is the financial value that owners can call theirs. The company owns the assets, the shareholders own the company and if all liabilities are paid off, using the assets (remembering that liabilities are 'outsiders' claims on the assets), then what is remaining belongs to the owners.

Equity can have a number of names, from 'owners equity' or 'owners capital' (generally both used when it's a small business) to 'shareholder equity' (or 'stockholder equity', depending on your location) when the business is a company with shareholders. Whatever you call it, just remember the above definition and the "residual interest" belongs to owners of the business.

If you look at the Equity section of Amazon's Balance Sheet you will find a number of different accounts listed. The reality is there are a vast number of account possibilities when it comes to Equity and unless you are a professional analyst or advanced accountant the truth is there are only a few you NEED to know about. We'll cover this now:

First, I want to combine two accounts for (a) simplicity, and (b) they may already be combined, depending on which country you reside. These accounts are 'Common Stock' and 'Additional Paid in Capital'. These accounts represent what shareholders have contributed in funds to the business when there have been equity capital raisings. So if a company doesn't want to get its money from debt finance it can turn to its shareholders to put in more cash in exchange for shares or stock in the business; they can contribute funds in return for partial ownership of the business. For example, if Amazon sells 10,000 shares at $10 each, then it should add $100,000 (10,000 x $10) to the total of this account.

The next important equity account is one that doesn't even appear in Amazon's balance sheet at year-end, or any balance sheet at year-end. This account is 'Current Earnings'. Current Earnings appears throughout the financial year and is the current years profit (or loss) at that point in time. So if the business' financial year runs from January till December and profits at the end of April are $5,000, then the equity account 'Current Earnings' in the balance sheet will show a figure of $5,000.

We are now addressing the account 'Retained Earnings' and we will also explain why Amazon doesn't have a current earnings account in the example balance sheet I've given you. Retained Earnings (or Deficit) are the accumulated retained profits (or losses) of the business since its inception. A profit in year 1 of $400 plus a profit of $300 in year 2 would lead to a retained earnings balance of $700 after both years. If you think about it, the literal translation of 'retained earnings' is kind of self-explanatory; it's the profit (earnings) since inception that has been kept (retained) in the business.

So why doesn't Amazon have a Current Earnings account? Well, depending on how the accounts are exactly prepared (I will use the simplest explanation), the current earnings balance (at year end when the final accounts are prepared) is closed off to retained earnings. That is, the current earnings balance is transferred to retained earnings; current earnings goes back to zero (because it's a new year with zero earnings for that year at that stage) and retained earnings is increased by the balance of current earnings (since now last years current earnings are effectively this years retained earnings). I just mentioned, "how the accounts are exactly prepared", I used this qualification because, according to Google Finance, Amazon never has a current earnings account, even in the quarterly reports. This could mean that Amazon (or Google Finance for simplicity) transfers current earnings to retained earnings every reporting period. However, this point is rather arbitrary, whichever way the balance sheet is presented to you, just know how what retained earnings is, and how any possible current earnings account is linked.

Before we leave the retained earnings account it's important to talk about dividends paid and where they fit into equity. While not on the Amazon balance sheet, all dividends a business makes are taken from the equity section. If you think about it, dividends are paid to shareholders so logically their recognition should also be from shareholders equity. Now, the exact accounting process can be done a few ways, but the key idea to remember is that all dividend amounts eventually come from retained earnings. Remember, retained earnings are profits kept in the business and dividends are paid out of profits, so effectively they are profits (earnings) NOT kept (not retained) in the business.

Before we leave equity, I'll just mention the 'Treasury Stock' account that Amazon has (as well as many other businesses) This accounts represents the value of shares, or stock, the company has purchased in its own business. If Amazon (as a corporation) purchases Amazon stock, the value of these purchases is placed in Treasury Stock. Companies often do this to immediately raise the value of their own shares or to return funds to stockholders without paying dividends (by buying their stock back from them possibly at a good price). In regards to immediately raising the value of the shares, if Amazon purchases its own shares it takes them off the market and reduces the supply of Amazon shares. All other things being equal, a reduced supply (and constant demand) will push up the price of the remaining Amazon shares.

51

Links between the Balance Sheet and the Income Statement (the Profit & Loss Statement)

The balance sheet and income statement are two of the three main financial statements (along with the cash flow statement), yet it is the balance sheet and income statement that are intricately linked. One reason behind this is the accounting concept of 'double-entry' accounting; a centuries old accounting practice where each business transaction affects at least two accounts. While double-entry accounting is the topic of another book, the two statements links may seem more logical if we look at one, simple example.

If Amazon sells a Kindle Book for $9.99 then logically 'sales revenue' (an income statement account) would increase by $9.99 but also their 'cash' balance (a balance sheet account) would also increase by $9.99. This simple illustration is just one of many examples of how accounts from one statement are linked to accounts in the other statement.

So, rather than detailing every possible example and eventuality, just remember that if you really want to develop your financial statement analysis skills then don't just stop with understanding the balance sheet. While I personally believe the cash flow statement is far underappreciated, overlooked and misunderstood, I still have to advise that, on your accounting knowledge journey, if you now only feel confident with the balance sheet then your next step should be learning about the income statement (the profit & loss statement). The two go hand in hand and when you are confident with both you will find 1 + 1 actually equals 3; the total benefit is greater than the sum of their parts.

There is one more major linkage example that I will discuss, briefly. This is actually something we have already covered, the feeding of earnings (or profit) from the income statement into the equity section of the balance sheet. Simply, last year's retained earnings (last years balance sheet) plus this year's profit (this years income statement) equals this year-end's retained earnings (this year end balance sheet). This is true forever and always, is one of the most understandable linkages and still one of the most important. It also provides a double-checking or feedback mechanism into how stable and accurate all your accounting systems are, remembering that the balance sheet must balance and profit must equal revenue minus expenses. Note: as discussed earlier, dividends affects retained earnings, so technically it is: last year's retained earnings (last years balance sheet) plus this year's profit (this years income statement) *minus dividends paid* equals this year end's retained earnings (this year end's balance sheet).

Conclusion

Well that's it! I feel great and I hope you feel the same way next time you come across a balance sheet. A famous Columbia University academic once told me that eventually you have to stop learning and start practicing. So while I thank you for wanting to learn about financial statements and purchasing this book, I urge you to take what you know now and start reading over as many balance sheets you can get your hands on. There is always room for more education (and with accounting you can spend a lifetime) but never forget to take the leap and spend more time analyzing your balance sheets. Ask questions of yourself when looking at the accounts and figures: "What is this telling me?" then "and if it says that, what is the next implication? And can I check that with information I already have?"

Too often accounting is seen as dry and boring, but accounting is the language of business and business is often our livelihoods; nothing this important should be written-off (an accounting phrase, haha) as dull or someone else's responsibility. Even if you never want to be an accountant, it's great that you are taking the steps so you need not rely on your accountant as heavily, can communicate better with them…and know if they are wasting your money. I hope this is the beginning of a great journey.

Finally, I identify myself as a businessperson as opposed to an author. So I hope, as a businessperson, this book has given you more value than your initial outlay of funds. Thanks for your purchase and your time in reading this book.

A picture tells a thousand words: how many words is your balance sheet telling you?

Best wishes!
Axel Tracy

Book 2: Income Statement Basics

Introduction

Whether you are running a business or analysing an investment, you will no doubt be provided with the financial statements of the business. These statements can be daunting if you are unsure about how to read them, yet it is imperative to have some accounting knowledge if you want to know the true state of a business. The financial statements, in short, give you a condensed glance into the financial success of any business.

While country-specific regulation dictates which financial statements must be prepared by an entity, the three key financial statements are:

1) The Income Statement (The Profit & Loss Statement)
2) The Balance Sheet (The Statement of Financial Position)
3) The Cash Flow Statement

This book will cover the basics of (1) The Income Statement, and will be part of a book series of all three of these statements.

This book is not aimed at accountants or financial advisors, it is aimed at those who are provided with financial statements, yet do not have an accounting background. Warren Buffett has said that accounting is the "language of business" so this book should hopefully teach you a few key 'phrases' that will allow you to converse about, and navigate around, the income statement. Will you become an expert from this book alone? No, but the beauty of the key financial statements is that even a basic level of knowledge will allow you to make leaps and bounds when it comes to extracting value from the statements; in this case, the income statement.

Hopefully you should be able to tear through this read in one or two sittings, and you'll be prepped to make better business and investment decisions the next time someone hands you an income statement.

All the basics will be covered in under 30 pages, so this is more of a bird's eye view than an in-depth, in-the-trenches account of the income statement. The way the book is structured is also pretty simple. Firstly, we give you a real-world example of an Income Statement, and then we talk about some housekeeping issues and key concepts behind the statement. Then the real-bones of the book begins: we talk about each individual line item of the income statement, some accounting behind the scenes and finally some inferences you can draw from the account figures.

I am educated in accounting…and not educated in writing! I write because I like to help people learn accounting concepts…and I am passionate about accounting! I mention this because while I'd love to be a best-selling author, I know I will never become a best-writing author. The best I can hope for is that I become a better writer through each book being published over time. You can help me achieve these two goals:

If you want to help me become a better writer, please email me at **axel@accofina.com** and give me your suggestions for
improvement.

If you want to help me become a best-selling author, please leave a positive review for this book (and maybe a comment on how it helped you) on Amazon.com or GoodReads.com.

Time to get cracking!

Have a look at the Income Statement on the next page, don't worry if it looks all too foreign at this stage, just try and grasp some of the components and key groupings; we'll cover the detail later. Just know that you can keep referring back to this example Income Statement as we progress and hopefully by the end of the book you will feel very familiar with what is going on.

Example Income Statement

Amazon, Inc. (NASDAQ:AMZN)
Consolidated Statement of Operations:
For 12-months Ending 31ˢᵗ December, 2012

Extracted from Amazon's 2012 Annual Report (page 38) that was found within the Investor Relations section of Amazon.com.

(In Millions of USD)

Income:

Net product sales	$51,733
Net service sales	$9,360
Total net sales	*$61,093*

Operating Expenses:

Cost of Sales	$45,971
Fulfilment	$6,419
Marketing	$2,408
Technology & content	$4,564
General and administrative	$896
Other operating expense (income)	$159
Total Operating Expenses	*$60,417*

Income from Operations $676

Interest Income	$40
Interest Expense	$92

Other Income (Expense), net ($80)

Total Non-Operating Income (Expense) ($132)

Income before Taxes $544

Provision for Income Taxes ($428)
Equity-method investment activity, net of tax ($155)

Net Income (Loss) *($39)*

Basic earnings per share ($0.09)
Diluted earnings per share ($0.09)

Weighted average number of shares outstanding:
Basic 453
Diluted 453

Consolidated Statement of Comprehensive Income: For 12-months Ending 31st December, 2012

Extracted from Amazon's 2012 Annual Report (page 39) that was found within the Investor Relations section of Amazon.com.

(In Millions of USD)

Net Income (Loss)   ($39)

Other Comprehensive Income (Loss):

Foreign Currency Translation Adjustments, net of tax	$76

Net change in unrealized gains on available-for-sale securities:

Unrealized gains (losses), net of tax	$8
Reclassification adjustment for losses (gains) included in net income, net of tax effect	($7)
Net unrealized gains (losses) on available-for-sale securities	$1

Total Other Comprehensive Income $77

Comprehensive Income $38

Housekeeping

Income Statement Formatting

The first housekeeping issue that is mentioned relates to the format of the Income Statement. The Amazon.com example statement just shown was drawn directly from their Annual Report, however you will find that different sources present the same information (the Income Statement) in different formats. So whether you are reading from annual reports, from Google Finance, from your broker or other information service, etc. you may find that each Income Statement is structured a little differently. Firstly, don't stress about this! You will soon have all the knowledge you need to navigate any format presented. I, for one, am used to reading Australian Income Statements, so Amazon.com being a US company and having US formatting forced me to take a 2nd look. But I, like you, didn't stress...the important idea is that whatever the format, in effect, the same information is being presented. There is still revenue at the top, followed by expenses and finally a bottom line being net income (profit). Just think of it being like the differences between American and British versions of the English language; sure there are some notable differences, but these wouldn't stop you communicating in either country.

Income Statement naming conventions

While formatting issues based on individual systems is kind of easy to explain away, the naming conventions of the Income Statement is a little more confusing. For whatever reasons, the name given to the Income Statement has changed many times (and rather rapidly too). You may find an Income Statement called 'a profit or loss statement', 'a profit and loss statement', 'a statement of financial performance', 'a statement of comprehensive income'…and even after researching this book and looking at Amazon.com's annual report: 'a consolidated statement of operations'. Just remember, whatever you name you come across, they are generally all the same thing. The national and international regulators just change the formal name (quite regularly), for reasons unbeknown to this author and many accounting professionals. The two most common names are 'income statement' & 'profit and loss statement' and if you are ever confused, just ask someone (or Google) if *that name* refers to an income statement or profit & loss statement. Apart from 'the statement of comprehensive income' (which we will address later), all names refer to exactly the same (I mean identical) document, it's simply a naming convention.

From here on in, and from the name of this book itself, we will be referring to it as the 'Income Statement'.

Brackets within financial statements and other accounting documents

Okay, this one may be obvious to you already, but since this is a 'fundamentals' book I thought it should be covered. If you look at the example Income Statement you will see some figures surrounded by brackets, e.g. ($39). In financial statements and accounting terminology, bracketed figures simply mean a negative value, i.e. minus $39. This means the corresponding figures are also subtracted in any further calculations, e.g. $100 + ($39) = $61. There is one qualification I must mention: if you look at the "Operating Expenses" section of Amazon's income statement, you will see there are no brackets in this sections figures. However, an expense's 'natural state' is a negative value (i.e. you always subtract expenses from income), thus when it explicitly states that a figure is an expense it may not have brackets surrounding it. The key idea is that if a figure in the income statement could be *either* a positive or negative value (e.g. Net Income), then brackets mean it is the latter: a negative value.

Quick Guide to the Income Statement

Explaining the Income Statement in a Few Paragraphs

Okay, so here comes the super-quick guide to the income statement that will act as a primer to the more in-depth analysis throughout the rest of the book.

The income statement is a performance report.

The income statement measures the performance of a business over a set time period based on its ability to earn profits over that set period.

While a balance sheet (another key financial statement) shows a snapshot picture in time, e.g. 21-Nov-2014, the income statement more closely resembles a 'video' as it measures performance over a set time period, e.g. 1-Jan-14 *through* 31-Dec-14. Note: the period need not be a year, it may be a month, quarter, half-year, etc.

How does it measure performance over set period?

Firstly it aggregates all sales and service revenue over the set period to create a 'revenue' figure.

Then it lists all the major expenses throughout the same period and groups them into easily understood accounts, e.g. admin expenses, marketing expenses, etc.

We then subtract the total expenses figure from the total revenue figure and what is remaining is that period's 'net income' (if the figure is positive) or 'net loss' (if the figure is negative). Ideally a business wants to have net income.

The benefits of income statement analysis are driven from how each line item, these being 'accounts' or sub-totals, shown in the income statement is used for further enquiry or action. For instance, you can analyse the ratio of net income to revenue to work out the profit margin, or you can analyse expenses over a number of income statements and see how expenses are growing or shrinking and make assumptions about management's cost control.

You may have just noticed how I mentioned that line items might be sub-totals (and not expense or income accounts). This is important to grasp as these sub-totals are also used for analysis. The idea is that the income statement is simply not just three lines: (1) revenue (2) expenses and (3) net income. Instead the income statement has a number of sub-totals throughout (although they can change depending on the format of the document). Common sub-totals include (and we will go through all these in detail later on): gross profit, operating income & income before tax. Even below the net income figure we may have more sub-totals and line items depending on the size of the organisation, with earnings per share data being the most common.

Accrual Accounting: A Vital Concept in Income Statement Analysis

The concept introduced here is the concept of 'accrual accounting'. This means (in short) that all revenue and expenses are measured when they are earned (revenue) or incurred (expenses) and this is NOT necessarily when the matching cash flows occurs. In other words, within the income statement there are 'non-cash items': revenue and expenses on the statement when no cash has changed hands. I'll give a quick example to hopefully help with the explanation.

Amazon.com pays its self-publishing authors 60-days after the end of the billing month, i.e. if you purchased this book in November, I as the author will be paid my royalty 60-days after the end of November (at the end of January). Now when should Amazon.com record this book's royalty expense? In November when the royalty expense was incurred (i.e. you buying the book and Amazon incurring the author royalty expense) or in January (most likely in the next year's accounting period) when the author royalty was actually paid?

The answer, under accrual accounting, is that the royalty expense for Amazon.com is recognised in November, when the expense was incurred. The idea behind this type of accounting is that the income statement is a measure of economic performance and not just cash performance. It makes more economic sense to record the royalty expense in November when the book was purchased and the author's royalty was incurred. In this case, cash payment is an arbitrary date set by Amazon.com itself and not reflective of economic reality. Accounting reports should always try and reflect economic reality and not arbitrary choices of management or outside actors.

In conclusion, the income statement uses accrual accounting and reports all revenue and expenses over a set accounting/time period and measures the economic performance of an entity in relation to its ability to earn net income (profits).

The Income Statement linking into Other Financial Statements

As mentioned in the introduction to this book there are 3 main financial statements: the Income Statement, the Balance Sheet and the Cash Flow Statement. One of the unique and advantageous qualities of these three statements is that they are all linked to one another and you can feed aspects of each into sections of others, both for calculation uses and for accuracy checking.

When it comes to the Income Statement, the Net Income figure links into the equity section of the balance sheet. Specifically, net income minus dividends equals this year's retained earnings increase. And last year's retained earnings (on last year's balance sheet) plus this year's retained earnings increase equals the new balance sheet figure for the next retained earnings account.

The other link to the balance sheet is more conceptual rather than arithmetic. You will see in the next sections there are formal definitions of income and expenses from the

International Accounting Standards Boards, or IASB. The IASB is an international rule-setter when it comes to financial accounting & reporting and when it comes to their definitions of income and expenses you will see that they are based on the definitions of assets, liabilities & equity and also on the rules of double-entry accounting. We will not delve into these issues now, but just remember that the formal definitions (of income and expenses) provided by the formal rule-setter (the IASB) are linked to the balance sheet concepts of assets, liabilities and equity.

Income

"Income is increases in economic benefits during the accounting period in the form of inflows or enhancements of assets or decreases of liabilities that result in increases in equity, other than those relating to contributions from equity participants"

- IASB Conceptual Framework 4.25(a)

Here is that IASB definition of income that was mentioned in that previous section. And while definitions of assets, liabilities & equity do not really fall in a book about the income statement, the key intake for a beginner from the above definition is "increases in economic benefits during the accounting period in the form of inflows". And breaking this down…and mind you, the IASB is famous for mind-bendingly convoluted prose…the definition of income is based on the idea of the accounting period (the length of the 'video' or set period) and the inflows or increase in economic benefits during this period, and 'economic benefits' can just normally be boiled down to 'money'.

As I'm writing this, I am beginning to question the benefit of including this definition in a 'basics' book. The IASB or FASB (the US equivalent) are at the top of the pyramid when it comes to the study of financial accounting, so I believe that their definitions are the purest source of knowledge. But when it comes to fundamental-level learning, the definition may make the concept more complicated than what it really is. So here is the solution: if the above definition (and possibly my explanation) is something you can grasp, then brilliant! If your eyes are glazing over and you are now less certain of your skill level than you ever were, then don't fear! Why, because here is the 'basic' concept: *Income is money you earn from selling goods or selling services (keeping in mind the accrual accounting concept).*

Lets get past definitions and look at real-world examples:

Turning back to the Amazon.com 'Income section' of the example Income Statement you will see "Net Product Sales $51,733" and "Net Service Sales $9,360". Simply, since the Income Statement's set period (accounting period) is the 12-months Ending 31st December, 2012, the line amounts shown, and just mentioned, mean that Amazon.com sold in the ordinary course of business $51,733m worth of products in the year, and note these are tangible ("touch-able") goods (products) like SLR Cameras, Bedding products, etc. And the 2nd line item, correctly referred to as an 'account' (so the 2nd income 'account' shown) simply means that Amazon.com sold $9,360m worth of services throughout 2012; services like subscriptions to Amazon Prime, streaming movies, etc. The difference being is that a 'service' is an experience, process or benefit that Amazon will offer or perform for you, while a 'product' is something Amazon will deliver to you. These are my definitions of product vs. service and I've modified them to apply to Amazon, so you may find different definitions for these depending on where you look. It's also important to note the goods and services lie on a spectrum. That is, at one extreme of the spectrum lie products that are tangible goods you receive in return for payment and the other extreme are services that are pure experiences offered by the seller's staff. In between, there can be different mixes of goods and services: think about an airline, they offer the service of transport but also offer products such as drinks and meals during that service. While this discussion may be somewhat off on a tangent, it does illustrate that the income statement often arbitrarily breaks down data into specific categories to allow comparability between all income statements.

Note: all the Amazon figures quoted above are "Net" figures, so it can be assumed that this is total sales less refunds, returns and other amounts reducing gross sales. And try to remember the 'accrual accounting' concept we talked about earlier.

A quick word on revenue: revenue is defined as income earned in the ordinary course of business. For example, a bookshop earns revenue selling books, but if that bookshop sold the company car for a profit, this may have earned "income" (the profit on the sale of the company car) but it wouldn't be classified as revenue as a company car sale is outside the ordinary course of business for a bookshop. In that case, the bookseller's car sale uses the accounting term 'gain' instead of revenue. The money received from the company car sale would be a $20,000 'gain'.

In reality, 'income' (in the top section of the income statement) and 'revenue' are often used interchangeably and, further, 'income' is often a shorthand way to say profit or net income, so it is important to look at the context as to how each of the phrases is used to understand which definition to apply.

So pulling this all together: The top section of the income statement (also known as the 'top line' by some journalists, analysts and others) lists the total sales revenue of the business in question over a set accounting period. The total sales revenue within the income section is often broken down into product and service distinctions and totals are given for all three: net product sales revenue, net service sales revenue and the aggregate total sales revenue or income. Underlying all this data is the concept of accrual accounting (described in the Quick Guide section), which means all the totals given refer to income *earned* in the period and *not* necessarily the cash received from sales.

Expenses

"Expenses are decreases in economic benefits during the accounting period in the form of outflows or depletions of assets or incurrences of liabilities that result in decreases in equity, other than those relating to distributions to equity participants."

- IASB Conceptual Framework 4.25(b)

Above is the definition of expenses according to the IASB and again it has links to the balance sheet even though expenses are within the income statement. The quickest way to make sense of this obtuse definition is to look at the similarities between it and the IASB definition of income in the last section. You will see rather quickly that the two definitions are mirrors of each other and the language is almost identical (it's just mirrored language). From this you can conclude that expenses are the opposite of income and essentially represent the opposite effect within the Income Statement, that being they subtract economic benefits (money) during an accounting period.

If again these definitions are not your preferred method of learning, the simplest way to look at it is that expenses are the ongoing costs to run the business during a set accounting period. They are things like office rents and marketing expenses. The things you need to pay for in the ordinary course of business. Using a basic definition again and mirroring the earlier statement, we can say that the 'basic' concept is: *Expenses are the monies you spend or incur while in the ordinary course of selling goods or selling services (keeping in mind the accrual accounting concept).*

Expenses take up most of the remaining Income Statement aside from the calculation results. That is, they lie beneath the income section and roll all the way down to the net income figure (aside from calculation results along the way).

Looking at a real-world example you can see Amazon's expenses (within the included Income Statement) include operating expenses, non-operating expenses and tax expenses (tax 'provisions' to be specific).

Before we go any further, it is time to talk about a number of different formatting options to describe how the expenses are set out in the income statement.

Alternative 1a 'Descriptive Format':

This alternative is just the option that Amazon.com has taken in our example. The descriptive format displays the revenue figure and simply subtracts all expenses to leave a net income figure.

You can see with Amazon.com that they have set out their Income Statement with an 'operating expenses' section that provides most of the detail of their day-to-day operations, which is directly below the revenue figures. Amazon divides their ordinary expenses into certain categories (such as Cost of Sales & Fulfilment) and simply allocates all ordinary expenses into one of these categories.

Note: It is often important to read the Notes to the Financial Statements (the 'fine print') to get further clarification into how the brief (1-page) set of results are calculated and allocated. After doing this with Amazon, I found out that they even break down their depreciation expenses into their respective operating expense categories, such as some depreciation for 'Fulfilment' and some depreciation for 'Technology & content', etc. Many businesses separate out depreciation and amortization and pool it as one expense and it was only through reading the fine print (the 'Notes') that I learned that Amazon used this particular accounting policy. Different accounting policies can have very wide implications for financial statement analysis, so the more comfortable you are with getting your head around the basics, the more you should delve into the financial statement 'Notes' to get even more detail.

Okay, getting back to topic, in short: the descriptive format shows revenue minus expenses equals net income.

Alternative 1b 'Functional Format':

The next common format is the functional format income statement. While essentially displaying the same information (all income statements essentially show the same thing), the functional format inserts a 'gross profit' section just below the revenue section. That is, revenue minus 'cost of sales' equals gross profit, and only then the rest of the expenses are listed.

The functional format separates out cost of sales and gross profit from all the other expenses. This format is common in retailing and manufacturing business (as 'cost of sales' play a large influence) while the descriptive format is more common in service businesses (as 'cost of sales' play a smaller role).

Here is a quick aside if you are unsure as to what 'cost of sales' are: Cost of sales, a.k.a. Cost of Goods Sold (COGS) or Cost of Revenue, are those expenses/costs which are incurred to get inventory that will later be resold. Perhaps in a retailing business cost of sales are the prices paid to wholesalers for the goods the retailer sells. Or perhaps in a manufacturing business, cost of sales are the costs/expenses incurred in manufacturing products that will later be resold.

Do you see why cost of sales and gross profit figures are vital indicators (and hence the use of the functional format) for businesses that hold inventory? Costs of Sales are unavoidable (and often large) expenses for some businesses so their measurement and ongoing management is very important. And gross profit figures (Revenue minus Cost of Sales equals Gross Profit) are also very important as they represent the starting point to meet all other expenses and net income.

Below the gross profit section, the descriptive format and functional format are the same. It is only the inserted gross profit section that makes the income statement a functional format statement.

Alternative 2a 'Single-step' format:

The 'Single-step' format is not an add-on from descriptive and functional formats, but is a separate format type to be compared to 'Alternative 2b Multi-step'. The 'Single-step' format is a description given to income statements that generally only offer one calculation (hence it's called single-step). This one calculation is revenue minus expenses equals net income. Thus the only sections that have aggregate totals are revenue and expenses and the single step is to calculate one minus the other.

These types of income statements are normally only used with smaller and more closely held businesses. The simpler style is adequate for smaller business or businesses without too many outside observers.

Alternative 2b 'Multi-step' format:

It is easier to understand alternatives 2a and 2b when you compare them to each other, so hopefully after you read this section the previous alternative will make more sense too.

The Multi-step format is what is used in the Amazon example income statement. It is a multi-step format statement because there are a number of calculations running down the page (hence, multi-step). Looking down the example statement now, you can see that revenue minus operating expense equals Income from Operations, then you subtract non-operating expenses to calculate Income before Tax and only after further subtracting tax expenses can you calculate a final Net Income figure. Do you see how this is multi-step? Each calculation down the page feeds into the next calculation.

Multi-step format statements are common in larger companies and especially those that are public companies and/or listed companies. This is because there is much more analysis that can be gleamed from a multi-step statement.

You can perform analysis and draw conclusions from any and all of the steps. This is beneficial when there are many outside parties who need to analyse the statements, for example when the company is listed on a stock exchange and there could be vast quantities of people interested in the details of the company income statement.

Alternative 3+ 'Management accounting' and other formats

While not as common as the other above alternatives, there are still a few other ways to format an income statement.

One you may come across is when expenses are broken down based on management accounting costing principles. For example, expenses can be broken down into fixed and variable costs. This example would be most useful for internal management when formatting isn't regulated at all. For reference, fixed costs are those that cannot be avoided in the short-term (hence they are fixed), variable costs are those that vary based on the level of production or activity (hence they vary and are called variable costs).

The key take-away from this alternative is that unless a format is dictated by a regulator or exchange, there is really no limit onto how you structure your own income statements. As long are there are revenue and expense sections and a final net income figure, you can design how to represent the statement. The important thing is that whatever format is chosen, it has to help the statement's reader make better business and investment decisions.

Operating Expenses

Now that we have dealt with a number of formatting options, let's return to the Amazon example we are working through. Understand one statement to begin with and branch out from there.

Directly below the revenue section you will find 'Operating Expenses'. Taking on board what was discussed earlier about expenses in general, operating expenses are those expenses that are incurred during the normal business operation. In Amazon's case, operating expenses would involve things like marketing the Amazon website with banner ads, or perhaps the cost of the servers that manage the Amazon website. You have to ask yourself: 'is this expense incurred during normal day-to-day Amazon management, that being the business of being an online retailer and technology service company?' When you can say 'yes' to this question then that expense will fall somewhere in the first expense section of 'Operating Expenses'.

Looking deeper, you can see the operating expenses are broken into categories. While I will not spend time by explaining the different between a 'Technology' expense and a 'Fulfilment' expense, the key take-away is the analysis that can be drawn from the category breakdown figures. You can see that Amazon's marketing expense is approximately half of the technology expenses; what can we draw from this?

Perhaps Amazon focuses on 'technological excellence' over 'marketing spin'? Or on the flip side, perhaps Amazon is giving up 'customer acquisition' and choosing 'technological fancies' instead?

In regards to which answer is which, I can't say, but what we can say now is that we have a starting point for filtering all Amazon Inc. company info we hear of from here. We also have benchmarks and proportions to measure against all future income statements, and see if there is a change in strategy (i.e. a deliberate cutting of costs, or growth in expenditure, in particular categories). We can also compare relative totals between Amazon and competitor companies, for example: perhaps we could infer that eBay Inc. has a bloated management structure if their 'General and Admin' costs were six times larger than Amazon's given similar revenue totals between the two (Note: I don't know the accuracy of this particular eBay/Amazon claim, it's just an un-researched illustration).

It's this type of analysis where we get the most value from income and other financial statement analysis. Now, don't get me wrong, there are limitations to what we can draw from an income statement alone, let alone when we start dealing with accounting manipulation. But from generally a single page document (or a few pages for all statements) you can't beat the succinct summarization that financial statements provide, and the guidance they offer for further inquiry. You have to keep asking yourself, "What is behind this figure?".

Remember that the income statement is a *summary* of the period, so ask yourself what the story may be behind each summarization.

Income from Operations

Now that we have the revenue data and the operating expenses data, we can calculate the Income from Operations. This is simply the former minus the latter. In the case of Amazon, it is $676m. Why is this result important? Simply: because this is the performance of the business at carrying out its core activities. Strip out the odds and ends, irregular occurrences and other financial complexities, the income from operations is simply how good Amazon was (in their case) at being an online retailer and technology provider for the previous twelve months. After all, isn't this something we want to know? You'd be a little concerned as an investor in Amazon if it constantly had accounting profits based on equity investment returns (for example) but could never get positive income from operations for being an online retailer. Sure you may not be too concerned as an investor if these accounting profits meant the stock price kept on rising, but still, you would most likely have invested in Amazon as an online retail and technology play and based your decision on Amazon putting itself out there as a leading retailer...not the (hypothetical) equity investment vehicle that is leading to its accounting profits.

Long story short: income from operations is a one-line performance measure about how well a business succeeded in running its core operations. This one line is not the whole story, but it's valuable to be aware of, keep an eye on, and understand.

Non-operating income and expenses

Remembering what we were just talking about in the last section, the next section of the income statement should be self-explanatory, or at least easy to grasp with a little explanation. Taking on board the concepts of revenue/income and expenses, non-operating income and expenses is simply those income and expenses that do not form part of the day-to-day, normal operations of the business.

You can see from Amazon's income statement that these non-operating entries involve interest income and expense as well as a catchall "other" account. Amazon isn't a financial institution, they don't 'normally' get involved in the business of borrowing and lending money; this isn't their day-to-day operations. But that doesn't mean they have zero interest income or expenses and we must account for these somewhere. So it falls into the non-operating income and expenses section. As for the catch-all "other" account, we can just assume that there are a number of other individually immaterial transactions that fall outside day-to-day Amazon business and are too small, or too widely dispersed to even categorize, except to put them in an "other" account.

Pulling these three accounts together, they are summed and presented with another one-line item: Total non-operating income or expense; in Amazon's case this is a loss of $132m. Now this one-line is not really that significant in itself, but where it draws most of its value is that this total is subtracted from Income from Operations to result in a more significant value, the one-line item Income Before Taxes.

Income Before Taxes

This total derives it's greatest use when you are an outsider and you are comparing multiple businesses, for example if you are analysing stock market investments and you have a choice of not only Amazon but also Wal Mart, eBay, Barnes and Noble and any other retailer, for example. While net income (after tax) is the "bottom line" of any business, you will find the tax liability and payments of any business will be slightly different to any other business. I'm not just talking about the total tax figure, but more about tax rates, tax credits, tax rollovers from previous years, etc. For almost each and every business tax complexities will be different each year and different between businesses.

Why does this have an impact? Because tax policy and tax rules are set outside the organisation. The governments set the rules and this is well beyond the control of management; those we are trying to assess with our income statement analysis. Further, if you as a stock analyst are trying to compare multiple companies in multiple countries, the tax rules and consequences on the "bottom line" can be like night and day across borders.

So if we are trying to assess the performance of a company and its management, shouldn't we strip out the parts of the income statement where management and the company have no control (e.g. Tax issues)? And this is what the Income Before Tax total provides: a profit figure measuring the performance of the business before things get complicated by outside taxation issues. Strip these complications out and you can now compare performances for companies in different tax jurisdictions, with a different tax status and with different tax implications.

Provision for Income Taxes

Move on to the next section of our income statement we will find the line item Provision for Income Taxes. In the simplest way to explain it, this is an expense that represents how much was allocated for income taxes this year.

It is a little more complicated than that quick explanation. For instance, this figure may not represent the final tax bill for that year. This is evidenced by the fact it is termed as a provision. In accounting terminology a "provision" is similar to a liability (e.g. a tax liability) but it isn't an 'exact' liability. As the IASB (the accounting rule-setters we talked about earlier) defines, a provision is a liability of uncertain timing or amount. Thus from this definition we can see that the provision for income tax relates to an uncertain amount or uncertain timing of payment. These two conditions fundamentally contradict the rules for recognizing a true liability, hence the provision concept.

Further complications into that simple definition include the fact that the figure doesn't represent how it was allocated, e.g. by way of putting away funds or actually paying taxes. The provision is just an accrual entry (remember accrual accounting from the Quick Guide section?) to recognise a probable debt that will eventually be paid. The figure is no guarantee or amount or timing of payment. The expense here is simply recognition that tax expenses are incurred in the same period as income is earned and also the opposite entry of balance sheet recognition of taxes owed within a double entry accounting system.

Lets not over complicate this line item, the simple definition will suffice and just further think about it as how much tax expense was incurred on the income the business earned in the year or accounting period. And a tax expense is like any other expense we discussed earlier except that it's paid to the government and not suppliers or employees. Anything deeper than this can be for your further studies beyond a 'basics' book.

Equity-method investment activity

This next section of our income is heavily influenced by accounting rules and terminology, so hang in there, as this line item can be quite substantial for some companies.

As you know many businesses invest and take stakes in other businesses. The example you are probably most familiar with is a subsidiary, i.e. this company is a subsidiary of that company or that company has this many subsidiaries. We are going to start our explanation with the parent, subsidiary concept and then move onto our current line item focus. A subsidiary is defined as a business in which a parent has 'control' over that subsidiary. 'Control' is the key concept here. The parent can ultimately dictate the financial and operating policies of the subsidiary and this is normally achieved through owning a majority of shares or having a majority of board seats. Now when a company has subsidiaries there are set rules on how to account for the subsidiaries' income, expenses, assets, liabilities and equity. These rules are called 'consolidation accounting' and in the end the financial statements of parent and all it's subsidiaries are blended together (in a quite complicated accounting procedure) to form one set of 'group' financial statements. In other words, from a quick glance of a group's income statement you can't see any specific line items for the subsidiaries. There is no line item or definition between parent and subsidiaries, they are blended to form a single set of statements.

Taking this on board now let's turn our attention to the line item equity-method investment activity. This is 2nd way to account for investments in other businesses. But these investments, shown within our current line item, are not subsidiaries where the parent has control. Instead we use this different accounting method (equity-method investment activity) when a company has 'significant influence' over another business. 'Significant influence' over the financial and operating policies of a company is the key criteria. And we don't call the influenced company a subsidiary, instead the accurate term is to refer to them as 'associates'. So in our example, the appearance of this line item proves that Amazon has an investment in at least one associate.

So what exactly is significant influence? How can we define this? Sadly, I can't give you a black and white definite answer. But a rough guide that normally holds true is when an investor company owns 20%-50% of the equity of the investee company. This normally allows significant influence over the 'financial and operating policies' of a company.

Still with me? Now let's get to that line item and its respective amount. When an investment in an associate is made, an asset on the balance sheet is created with the value of the cost of that investment. For (hypothetical) example, Amazon buys 30% of company ABC for $1 million, therefore on the Amazon balance sheet an asset (with a $1 million value) is recognised on the Amazon balance sheet. Over time company ABC makes profits, losses, pays dividends, etc. which all affect the equity of company ABC. While the exact accounting behind it is complicated and beyond the scope of this book, all these changes in company ABC's equity are proportionally transferred to the asset that Amazon recognises on its balance sheet. For example, if company ABC made $200,000 profit (an increase in equity) in 2015, then the Amazon asset would increase by 30% times $200,000 or $60,000.

We are almost there: so, finally, what is represented on the income statement of Amazon (we've been talking lots about assets and balance sheets)? The figure on the income statement is simply Amazon's share of the change in equity of its associates (remembering that income is increases in assets matched with increases in equity). Simply collect the net equity changes of all Amazon's associates (that have led to the net change in Amazon's associates assets on its own balance sheet), multiply these equity changes by Amazon's ownership share, sum/aggregate all these and we at last have the figure of a $155m loss.

So, while the concept and accounting behind is a little harder to grasp, understanding this investments and the line item is important. Considering Amazon's income before tax was $544m, a $155 loss from its associates is a pretty hefty slap. And depending on the strategy of any particular company, its investments in associates could be much greater with an even greater exposure to potential losses or gains.

Net income (loss)

Okay, here we are almost finished! We have reached the net income figure. This figure is the company's profit, its net income: the bottom line, as it often referred to as.

While the concept of profit as defined by the international accounting standards board is more complicated than it needs to be, the more digestible idea is that profit, or net income, is simply income (revenue and gains) minus expenses. And these details are exactly what we have been going through in this book. So in Amazon's case, we take the income before taxes figure and subtract the income tax expense and the equity-method accounting expense to achieve a net loss (the figure is in brackets) of $39m.

Net income is the simplest and purest measure of performance. It is a summary of all the businesses activities for the period wrapped up in a single figure. And when the "profit motive" is the fundamental goal of corporate entities in a capitalist system, you can see why net income becomes the "bottom line" when it comes to the performance of the business. Note, the term "bottom line" is synonymous with being a representation of what's "most important" for many aspects in everyday life, it's easy to forget that the term is based on the accounting income statement and the net income figure normally resides on the actual bottom line on the page/statement.

So now that we have this figure, what can we do with it? Like many financial statement items, it's best value can be drawn from comparison with other items of financial statements, both current and past statements. Although it is important to note that no other figure on the income statement can quite stand alone as a source of informational value as the net income figure can, as there is much we can do with knowing this figure without reference to other data.

So let's get to the point, what can we do with this figure? We can assess the trend in performance by looking at previous net income figures; is this figure increasing steadily over time? Or do we have a 'growth' company and it's increasing rapidly? Ideally, unless management made a conscious decision to scale back in size, we wouldn't want this figure falling over time. I mention this often, but it's important to use key pieces of data as not ends in themselves, but the grounding for further inquiry. So using some sort of trend analysis as an example, we may next inquire into what has changed, or remained the same, over the period of analysis.

For example, if the net income trend has stopped increasing and has now fallen, ask yourself why might this be so. Is there new strong competition? Have the general economic conditions changed? Has a new management strategy backfired? In short, listing every possible reason for a hypothetical change in net income trend is a limitless and a little futile. Just remember that a valuable piece of data can become more valuable when compared against similar data in different periods and that individual figures are of great use for further enquiry.

Other comparison relationships that can make the individual figure more valuable is when you compare the net income figure to similar businesses or competitors within the industry. You can see if any particular measure of performance is inline with everyone else, and thus not really that unique or special, or whether it stands out from the crowd and represents something unique about that particular business and is worth further investigation.

The next technique you can use has been mentioned earlier. You can compare the net figure to other line items within the financial statement, whether this is the income statement itself or the balance sheet or the cash flow statement. There are particular ratios, such as the profit margin (net income divided by sales revenue), that are common within financial statement analysis, but the honest truth is that there is no real limit on what ratios you can calculate and which you put emphasis on. If you can justify value from the ratio of net income to another piece of data, then there are no rules against doing this. While the common ratios have become mainstream because of their regarded value to analysis, it is unique information that may give you an edge over others: as no one else may have this particular insight. Just make sure that before you run off placing too much emphasis on any ratio (this could apply for any analysis technique) that you test the relationship with your desired outcome and perhaps give it time and multiple occurrences before you risk too much of your investments or business on it. As with many pursuits, you need to try things in the real world to become skilled, but make sure you can walk before you run.

So get out there, start walking and start applying some analysis techniques using the net income figure, but as for this book we are going to move onto the EPS and shares outstanding data which sits after the net income figure.

Earnings per Share Data

This section of the book actually focuses on the next four pieces of data (or line items) below the net income figure, as opposed to just a single piece of data. We are now looking at Basic earnings per share, Diluted earnings per share and the two lines incorporating 'weighted average number of shares outstanding' (both basic and diluted).

For many investors the absolute net income figure, which we just discussed, is not too easily distinguishable and valuable without some of the deeper analysis we talked about. Often as investors, when we need a more distinguishable figure, or more of a headline figure, and for this we can look at earnings per share (EPS) data. This figure represents a quick and handy glance at what our shares (ownership) did for a particular period. We, as share owners after all, want to know what earnings we're generated on each share. The EPS data gives us this information. It is a quick and simple calculation that allows comparison against all possible stock market opportunities (that is, all stock market companies offer EPS data so we can easily compare all investment opportunities).

You will also find that EPS data is what most of the major media company's report in their stories. Whether it's Bloomberg or the Wall Street Journal or any other, you will find that they generally report company earnings via an EPS figure. This feature alone makes it imperative for any investor to become familiar with this piece of data.

Further, many professional stock market analysts (those that provide company forecasts and reports, buy or sell recommendations, etc.) base their earnings estimates using an EPS figure. For example, you often here something like this is the financial media: "the consensus earnings estimate for company XYZ this quarter is $1.27 a share". This is simply another way of saying that the forecast EPS is $1.27. Due to the significant stock price changes that can be caused by meeting, beating or missing analyst forecasts, it becomes even more important to understand EPS figures.

The final aspect I will mention before moving onto our Amazon example is that there is a relationship between EPS data and stock prices. While it is different in every single, individual company case, it can be generally said that the higher the EPS figure, the higher the stock price. Due to the fact that stock investors are indirectly purchasing a claim to the earnings of a business when they purchase shares, it is no accident that shares with higher earnings attached to it (i.e. higher EPS) fetch higher prices in the stock market. If I quote exact data today it may become stale in a book without exact date references, but I will say, if you want proof of this general rule, go to Google Finance online and pick a stock with a price less than $10 and find its EPS data, then go look up Berkshire Hathaway Inc. 'A' Shares and see what it's stock price is and its respective EPS data. What you will find is no accident and will be, in general, repeated throughout the stock market in varying degrees.

Okay, let's move onto how EPS data & 'weighted average number of ordinary shares outstanding' are calculated and then how this applies to our Amazon example.

Simply, EPS is calculated by dividing net income by the (convolutedly named) weighted average number of ordinary shares outstanding. Basic earnings per share is Net Income divided by Basic weighted average number of shares outstanding and Diluted earnings per share is Net Income divided by Diluted weighted average number of shares outstanding. Not to difficult, huh?

Weighted average number of shares outstanding isn't too difficult to grasp either. It is simply a calculation of the average number of shares outstanding over the year (or period). Because new shares may be issued, or shares bought back or cancelled, the number of shares outstanding often fluctuates up and down over a year. To take account for these fluctuations, the figure and term, weighted average number of shares outstanding was created to give an average number of shares outstanding. It is 'weighted' because each level of shares outstanding may last for different lengths throughout the year. The weights represent the portion of the year for each level of shares. For example, there may be 1000 shares outstanding in January and then on the 1st of February 200 new shares are issued and the number of shares outstanding remains at 1200 over the rest of the year. In this example we can make a calculation to determine the Weighted average number of shares outstanding: 31 days at 1000 (all of January) and 334 days at 1200 shares outstanding (the rest of the year). Thus the calculation with applying weights is 31/365 times 1000 plus 334/365 times 1200. The result is 1183 and therefore in this example the weighted average number of shares outstanding is 1183.

Now to the terms 'basic' and 'diluted': Basic refers to the

number of current, standard level of shares. The diluted level refers to the number of shares outstanding if all stock options or convertible bonds were exercised. For example if there were 1000 basic shares outstanding but the CEO of the company had stock options that entitled her to 300 shares (if exercised) then the diluted level of shares outstanding would be 1,300.

So now we have covered all the fundamentals, we can look at the Amazon example. The first thing you'll notice is that basic and diluted weighted average number of ordinary shares outstanding is the same. While this makes it easier for us to understand our example, this situation is often not the case. Anyway, knowing this we can look at our example income statement and see the Net Loss of $39m divided by 453m weighted average number of ordinary shares outstanding results in the basic and diluted EPS of ($0.09).

Quick Summary & Lead into Comprehensive Income Statement

Well, we have now finished with our core analysis of the income statement, well done! You could finish your reading here and be adequately prepared to work your way around a small business income statement or still perform a lot of analysis of the income statement of a listed company. We've basically covered the tried and tested fundamentals of income statements. I hope you get out there and start looking through more and more income statements and apply what you have learned and start developing your own systems of analysis.

There is still one more section to this book, though. In recent times, the financial accounting standard setters have added another section to the income statement. This new section is a little complicated conceptually, but thankfully if you do struggle here… or I struggle to explain it well, I can assure you that what we have covered so far in this book will keep you in good stead for the large majority of occasions when you need to understand the income statement. This new section is the Statement of Comprehensive Income which is included after our example main Amazon Income Statement. The Statement of Comprehensive Income comprises changes in 'Other Comprehensive Income' or OCI. So, if you are ready and want to complete the final step of this introductory journey, let's get to it!

Other Comprehensive Income (OCI)

Other comprehensive income and this measure of performance now needs to be reported for large or important companies ('reporting entities') either in a separate statement in itself or as part of a Statement of Comprehensive Income. In the Amazon example, they have chosen to include a 'Consolidated Statement of Comprehensive Income' directly after their income statement. This statement reports the changes in other comprehensive income (OCI).

What:

So what is OCI? It is actually a little difficult to summarize in a nice, neat fashion. It can encompass a number of different items, but essentially all items in OCI "reflect re-measurements as a result of movements in a price or valuation". What does this mean? In general, apart from a few exceptions, assets or liabilities of the company can and often do get revalued as part of the accounting process. The financial accounting standard setters decided that these revaluations may not be *real* gains or losses to be shown in the main income statement, but should instead be recorded as gains or losses in a catch-all section which is OCI.

Here's where it gets even trickier: some "re-measurements as a result of movements in a price or valuation" DO, in fact, go into the main income statement, some do not (and instead go into OCI) and some go into OCI and are then 'recycled' or transferred into the main income statement at a later date….confused? Yeah, me too. And we are not alone: even the financial accounting standard setters, the mighty rule writers at the top of the pyramid, cannot give a definite answer about which revaluations ("remeasurements") appear where. Some situations are easier to understand than others (I'll give a quick example in the 'Why' section next) but if at this introductory level you need something to hold onto, then the best answers is to read the titles of the individual line items, remember that they are the double-entry accounting treatment of "movements in price or valuation" in assets or liabilities and then try to play devil's advocate of why they are not included in the main income statement. Remember they are all accounting treatments, and those within the organisation ultimately decide all accounting policy and treatments, so the rule setters have limited the accounting policy choice of some internal managers (or internal accountants) to avoid perverse incentives.

Why:

I just said OCI has been used to avoid perverse incentives of internal managers. This is only partly true and definitely not the full truth. The truth is that accountants are supposed to be conservative. No, that's not only a funny stereotype, they are supposed to "anticipate no profit and provide for all possible losses". Accountants are supposed to be the cold shower for the CEO's hopeful optimism. Okay, take this board as step one.

Step two, let's again look at the formal definition of income we defined early in this book, *"Income is increases in economic benefits during the accounting period in the form of inflows or enhancements of assets or decreases of liabilities that result in increases in equity, other than those relating to contributions from equity participants."* That is, income represents increases in equity from increases in assets or decreases in liabilities.

Final step: ultimately we must account for *anything* that fits that definition of income. And in complex entities with complex accounting there are a number of activities that do, in fact, fit this definition but breach the conservatism principle or do not otherwise truly represent management's use of company resources. For example, if company ABC on the NYSE held stock in a speculative, micro-cap company that doubled in value in one day, would that be *real* income for ABC? Did management have any control over the quick spike in this asset's value? ABC's assets and equity did both go up over that one day! Some conservative accountants might argue this is NOT real income until ABC actually *sold* the stock at the new value and *realised* the income.

This previous example of income (or losses) is just one of many that can fit the formal definitions of income or expenses but fail the conservatism test of being *real* or fail to truly represent management decisions. And yes, there can be losses in OCI, they are just the same circumstances as OCI income but reversed. And because there are so many possibilities of these *unreal* income and expenses, OCI was created. OCI is hoped to show ALL transactions that fit the definition of income and expense, but aren't allowed to be shown in the main income statement (or is conservative not to show in the income statement).

Ideally, the inclusion of the OCI section in a complete income statement is supposed to give a broader picture over the performance of the entity, even if outside management control. The OCI data is included if it is relevant to helping make better decisions based on the Income Statement.

Here's another quick example to show why some income isn't allowed to be shown in the main income statement. This is the example in 'Why' I referred to earlier and also one that is aimed at avoiding perverse incentives:

Earlier we talked about company ABC owning a speculative stock, but as speculative or small cap as it might be, if it's a listed stock then at least there is a public price that is hard to argue with. Let's now imagine company XYZ that owns 5 office buildings. Under a particular accounting rule, company XYZ may revalue these office buildings on the balance sheet up to 'fair value' when fair value is higher than the current 'book value' (the value the office buildings as currently stated on the balance sheet). Now this isn't a formal definition of this particular accounting rule, but we can still continue with the argument: what is 'fair value' of these 5 office buildings? There is no public exchange to get accurate prices, there could be multiple values dependent on which appraiser values the buildings, and some buildings may have steel foundations while all other comparable buildings may have concrete foundations. You see what I'm getting at here? The ultimate determinant of what fair value to put on these buildings is up to company XYZ's accountant…part of internal management! What if company XYZ was about to miss analyst earnings forecasts of $1m? Wouldn't it be easy for company XYZ's accountant to revalue the office buildings up by $2m? Assets go up $2m (the increase in "fair value" of the buildings), equity goes up $2m as the double-entry balancing adjustment, and voila (!) net income goes up $2m (remember the formal income definition) and company XYZ beats the analyst earnings forecasts! This is a rather simple demonstration but you'd be surprised how often it occurred until the financial accounting standard setters dictated that this type of income under the revaluation model (that particular accounting rule) must be recognised in OCI instead of net income. Specifically, assets would still go up $2m but the double entry balancing adjustment *must* go in an OCI equity account (called revaluation surplus) instead.

Detail:

Okay, in this 'Detail' section I am only going to give a brief overview. I will try and make the overview comprehensive in scope, but the analysis will not be deep. A deep, detailed tutorial would in effect become an advanced financial accounting course. I will give you a list of most possible items in OCI and the go through the Amazon example that only touches on a few of the possibilities. My best advice: if this 'Detail' section confuses you and you want to know more or if this section's analysis is not deep enough, then please let this be an invitation to further your accounting knowledge journey. The Internet, other more advanced books and educational institutions all offer deeper, more advanced and often better education than this book. So let me be brief in this section and, if desired, continue your knowledge journey with new sources.

When I first learned about other comprehensive income (OCI) it involved taking a couple of particular accounting courses within a degree and studying the Accounting Standards

Handbook which is a 1600+ page book detailing the rules of the IASB (no, we didn't have to read the book cover to cover in our courses). What I did learn though was that there is no specific list, no index item or section that was solely focused on OCI. Instead, rules for using OCI were spread sporadically throughout the whole Handbook. So when I approach writing this section in this book I cannot reference an exact list of all items that fall within OCI. What I have found though is a couple of good websites (**www.ifrsbox.com** & **www.accountingtools.com**) that both do indeed try and give a direct list. So here is a blended list of their offerings.

According to these websites, which I tend to agree with, this is an itemized list of all accounts that could appear in the OCI section:

1) Available-for-sale securities fair value changes that were previously written down as impaired
2) Available-for-sale securities unrealized gains and losses
3) Debt security unrealized gains and losses arising from a transfer from the available-for-sale category to the held-to-maturity category
4) Foreign currency gains and losses on intra-entity currency transactions where settlement is not planned or anticipated in the foreseeable future
5) Foreign currency transaction gains and losses that are hedges of an investment in a foreign entity
6) Gains and losses arising from translating the financial statements of a foreign operation

7) Changes in revaluation surplus related to property, plant and equipment

8) Actuarial gains and losses

9) The effective portion of gains and losses on hedging instruments in a cash flow hedge

10) For financial liabilities designated as at fair value through profit or loss: fair value changes attributable to changes in the liability's credit risk

Note: This is not my own list. It is a blend of two lists from the websites listed above. I have provided these links for you for your own review. These websites offer a 'good option' when trying to offer you, the reader, a comprehensive list when this list is not offered in the Handbook.

With that qualification note covered, and the list given, you will see why I am not going into each item in detail. A detailed discussion is simply beyond the scope of an introductory level and would break the short, concise format I want this book to hold. I encourage you to research, study or simply Google each item on your own: best wishes.

Now for the Amazon example, where I will briefly cover some of the detail: Let's look at our Amazon Consolidated Statement of Comprehensive Income. All of those listed items in the Amazon example really only cover Item (2) and Item (6) from our just mentioned 'exhaustive' list. Let's go through the comprehensive income statement one by one.
Firstly, Amazon begins with the Net Income figure of a $39m Loss taken from the main profit or loss statement that we covered, it then moves onto the OCI section.

First up, it talks about Item (6) "Gains and losses arising from translating the financial statements of a foreign operation" or as Amazon puts it "Foreign Currency Translation Adjustments, net of tax". This amount (of $76m) occurs because balance sheet items (assets, liabilities and equity) of foreign operations are translated at different foreign exchange rates than income statement items. Some parts of the income statement (such as tax provisions, depreciation and OCI) are reliant on balance sheet items while we are trying to present income statement items in this section. If you translate foreign currencies at different rates and at different times, the equality link between the balance sheet and the income statement is broken. No longer does last period's equity plus income (minus losses) equal this period's equity. When breaking this equality breaks accounting rules then a new temporary 'trick' balancing account is added: Foreign Currency Translation Adjustments. This is ultimately a 'nothing' account other than a dummy account to make sure all accounting rules hold after foreign currency conversions (translations) have taken place. It is just a balancing account in the balance sheet and it can change the value of balance sheets items and thus sometimes creates formally defined income or expenses. Therefore since it does create formally defined income or expenses, it must be shown somewhere in comprehensive income.

The next section Amazon has is "Net change in unrealized gains on available-for-sale securities". This section (thankfully) is a little more self-explanatory, in fact we sort of covered it in our company ABC example just a short while earlier.

First, we have the account: Unrealized gains (losses), net of tax, of $8m. This is simply unrealized (unsold) gains or losses of securities that are held by Amazon that are available for sale (or, could be sold at any moment without restriction). So a stock listed on the NASDAQ possibly held by Amazon would be available for sale as there is a ready market for these investments and nothing restricting any possible sale, while a security in an unlisted company (perhaps share capital in startup) may not be available for sale as there is no liquid market for this of security, in effect its sales is restricted.

Next up in the "Net change in unrealized gains on available-for-sale securities" section we have: Reclassification adjustment for losses (gains) included in net income. This account is a reversal of the previously discussed account for security gains or losses which *have* been realised, i.e. the securities have been sold, the income becomes 'real', is taken out of OCI and then transferred to the main income statement. So, hypothetically, if the following year all those unrealized gain securities (remember it was $8m) were sold the following for $10m, then the following year's "reclassification adjustment" would be a gain of $8m (which would be in brackets: see the line item and formatting description in the example statement) and the actual $10m gain would be in the main income statement, as described by this particular line item.

From here all the remaining items in the Statement of Comprehensive Income are totals and summations, and thus are pretty easy to grasp.

Firstly, we have a total of the "Net change in unrealized gains on available-for-sale securities" which is simply the sum of the previous two totals which we ran through.

Next up we have a Total of Other Comprehensive Income, which is just a sum of Foreign Currency Translation Adjustments and Net change in unrealized gains on available-for-sale securities. This is the total (given by the name) of the 'mini' income statement that is the Statement of Comprehensive Income.

And finally we have a total that is the bottom line of the main income statement plus the total of other comprehensive income.

This Comprehensive Income figure is the final line item on our full, comprehensive income statement.

Conclusion

Well, that's it! We've covered the general income statement and briefly gone over the statement of comprehensive income. You are now armed with the core knowledge to begin income statement analysis, congratulations!

Thank you for your purchase of this book and thanks even more for the time you have given to reading it. I do hope you feel confident with what we have gone through and you are now more prepared when you come across your next income statement. I have enjoyed writing this concise book, but the true value is the belief that I have helped you on your accounting knowledge journey, or even helped you start it. I will say that like a lot of other subjects, with financial statement analysis you learn the most when not only studying but also when applying what you have learned. There are an enormous amount of free sources of income statements out there, especially on the internet, so make sure that you believe in yourself and have a crack at performing some income statement analysis. No one has perfect knowledge: not you now, not me ever, nor my accounting professors, but this should not stop any of us from applying, testing, refining and repeating what we know about financial statement analysis. This book has hopefully given you the belief that you are now ready to start your own analysis and system development.

Thanks again, best wishes and I'll leave you with a quote from one of my idols, Warren Buffett: "Time is the friend of the wonderful business, the enemy of the mediocre." It's now time to use the income statement as part of your determination into which side of this quote your target business falls within.

Best of success!

Axel

Book 3: Cash Flow Statement Basics

Introduction

Welcome to the final instalment of the Financial Statement Basics series: Cash Flow Statement Basics.

The cash flow statement is probably the most underestimated (and often most ignored) of the three main financial statements. Yet its power to outline the status of a business is truly astonishing! It can tell you the stage of the business within its lifecycle or the strategy taken by management or even the success (and viability) of a business as a going concern.

Within this brief book, you will learn how to extract all this information (and more) from any cash flow statement you come across.

There are a few changes in this instalment that will be outlined soon, but you will find that Cash Flow Statement Basics follows a similar path to Balance Sheet Basics and Income Statement Basics with the same conversational tone and once again looking at the real-world financial statements of Amazon Inc.

So what exactly is this book about? It's about learning how to navigate and understand the cash flow statement. The cash flow statement, along with the income statement and the balance sheet, are the three main financial statements produced by a financial accounting system. The financial statements are concise, accounting theory driven summaries of a business and its activities over a period of time or at a particular point in time.

Financial statements are used by both those outside and inside the business to get a birds-eye view of all the financial activity of a business. Within this financial activity you can trace a story about what is going on inside the business, and if you can do this 'story-telling' well then you, as an investor or manager, can make intelligent decisions about how to move forward with your investment and business decisions.

Each of the three main financial statements serves a different purpose in telling the story. The balance sheet, through its assets, liabilities and equity, allow you see through one window. The income statement, with its revenue, expenses and profit, let you look through another window and see a different angle. The cash flow statement offers yet another view and its purpose is to trace the cash in the business: where it came from and where it left. This is done through the classification of operating, investing and financing cash flows.

Like I have said in previous books, while the study of accounting can take a lifetime to master, the fundamentals are not too difficult to grasp. And even a basic understanding of accounting will often dramatically change how you approach your business or investments. It will also put you in a very select group; my accounting lecturers often remind us that there is an extreme lack of accounting literacy in the business world. Thus just a short investment in accounting education will immediately ramp you up to an upper percentile.

I wish you the best over the coming pages and offer my thanks for giving this book the time that you are now.

Naming Conventions

As in previous titles, I would like to give notice that the financial statements often have various naming conventions. Thankfully, the cash flow statement naming conventions are nothing like the balance sheet or (worse yet) the income statement.

The main alternative name for the cash flow statement is 'the statement of cash flows' or in a large corporate group, 'consolidated statement of cash flows' (because the financial statements have been consolidated within a group of companies). You may also see it referred to (or really shortened to) simply as 'cash flow', as it's titled in Google Finance.

Formatting

I am writing this book from Australia, while looking at the cash flow statement of a US listed company from an financial data website. Thus, almost all these factors become variables when it comes to how I am presented with the actual statement. I.e. business location, business size or structure, source of the statement or even finance department preference all result in particular cash flow statement formatting. In fact, the IASB (the international accounting rule setters) and resulting IFRS rules allow the particular presentation of the statement to be based on individual business appropriateness, rather than a dogmatic structure.

But all these differences are superficial and particular peculiarities within these variables can simply be seen as different accents within the same language. That is, if you went to the UK (from the US) the locals would sound different but they are still speaking English. Your initial interaction with the dialect may be a little confusing, but it wouldn't stop you conversing, and soon enough the accent would be imperceptible. So yes, you will come across various formatting conventions of the cash flow statement, but they are all using the same accounting language and they are all saying the same thing.

So if you are brand new to accounting: don't stress! Treat any new format something like a new website you're browsing: scan the statement quickly from top to bottom, bottom to top, look for headings and emphasised text and even look at the numbers and try and find any logic in the arithmetic. I'm sure you'll be 100% fine, in fact it's really not that confusing at all; I'm even thinking this section is a bit of overkill (as I write it) considering how much time I've spent discussing it.

What's Different from Previous Titles in this Series?

While the second title in this series (Income Statement Basics) was very similar in structure to the initial title (Balance Sheet Basics), in this third and final title I wanted to make some major changes in the structure. Thus I thought it would be best to include this section near the start of the book to both acknowledge the shift in structure and that there is a lack consistency in this final title from the first two. I wanted to 'warn' readers of the previous titles that there will be some changes and to explain my reasoning behind this.

Increased use of Sub-Headings and Sub-Sections

Let's start the changes immediately, ha! You will find that this title will be less long prose and more bite-size lessons. I wanted to make it less like a 'novel' that is read like a story from beginning to end and more like a tutorial where you can jump back and forth from section to section and highlight or take notes with easily-identifiable references to where the notes were sourced from.

Working from Example Statement Bottom-to-Top and not Top-to-Bottom

In the earlier titles I referred to real-world Amazon Inc. financial statement and worked through it, line by line, from top to bottom. In Cash Flow Statement Basics I will be working through the statement in reverse: from bottom to top.

I have done this for two reasons. First, the more complex section rests at the top, in terms of the different formatting of the cash flow statement. Thus, I would like to work you into it slowly before blasting you with the hardest part first.

Secondly, the life cycle of a business normally begins with activity in the bottom section of the cash flow statement. Thus, it seems more logical, in a real-world chronology, to begin at the bottom of the statement.

Section Structures Repeat Throughout

I will explain my reasoning for this change before explaining this change directly. My most successful book has been Ratio Analysis Fundamentals. This title (which is outside this particular series) has far outsold any book I have written to date. This apparent success is something I cannot explain definitively even to this day. It's surprising, as I would have thought that books on financial statements would have much broader appeal than the more niche topic of ratio analysis. The biggest suspicion I have as to why readers have preferred Ratio Analysis Fundamentals, and my hypothesis from here, is that the book is very much structured as a tutorial that has a set format and repeating structure throughout, with only particular ratios and respective content changing through the book. Thus, I will by trying to replicate this repeating, course-like structure.

So, you will quickly see in this book that each section of this book is rather similar to the last. Only the particular section of the cash flow statement and the respective section content will change. This change feeds into the earlier 'Sub-Heading and Sub-Section' change; I would like this book to be more like a brief readable course with actionable lessons throughout. Accounting (for many) is hardly the most thrilling topic to read about, so I would like this book to be more tutorial-like where readers can apply learned skills after reading particular content.

More Analysis Sections and Less Accounting Theory

The previous two books followed a structure where the example financial statement was explained line by line with accompanying lessons on particular accounting theory that led to that particular line item or account.

Cash Flow Statement basics discusses less of this accounting theory (behind each line item) and focuses more on conducting analysis that may be behind some of the cash flow statement results.

While this is only on 'basics' book and thus cannot conduct a comprehensive guide to analysis for every possible outcome, I'm hoping this new focus may be more practical for you and other readers rather than being too theoretical in nature.

The Cash Flow Statement in a Few Paragraphs

Before we spend the remainder of the book diving into the cash flow statement, I would like to very briefly explain the statement in only a few paragraphs. Ideally this will give you a guide into where we are going and also provide quick primer as we approach each section.

So what is the cash flow statement? Simply, it tells us about cash inflows and outflows of a business over a length of time. Further, it categorises cash flows into particular business activities that give the statement reader further insight into the status of the business, whether it's performing successfully, whether it's expanding or winding down or whether it's raising cash among other things.

A standard cash flow statement will show a net change in cash over the period. It may only show this net change or it may show a cash starting balance, an ending balance and thus also the resulting net change.

This net change in cash is also broken down into three main (and standard) categories. These are cash flow from operating activities, cash flow from investing activities and cash flow from financing activities.

Cash Flow from Financing Activities

From latter to first: cash flow from financing activities displays all cash inflows and outflows that have to do with how the business is financed. That is, how it raises cash from external parties to fund the business (inflows) and how it then returns cash to those who funded the business (outflows).

Cash Flow from Investing Activities

In the second section, cash flow from investing activities, details of all cash inflows and outflows are outlined in respect to investments and sales of non-current assets. These are the long-term assets of the business that normally generate the income of the business.

Cash Flow from Operating Activities

This section of the cash flow statement details the nuts and bolts of the business. That is, this section outlines cash inflows and outflows of the day-to-day operations of the business.

For example, if the statement is for a bookstore, then the cash flow from operations would detail money coming in and out in the process of actually selling books. You could contrast this with selling shares to raise the cash to open a bookstore (cash flow from financing activities) and spending funds on buying a retail space to sell books (cash flow from investing activities).

Cash Flow Equation

While there is no formal detail of a cash flow equation in the statement, I thought it might be handy to outline how you calculate the net change in cash given in the statement. It is simply:

Cash at Beginning of Period

+ Cash Flow from Financing Activities

+ Cash Flow from Investing Activities

+ Cash Flow from Operating Activities

= Cash at End of Period

And thus 'Net Change in Cash' is simply:

Cash at End of Period – Cash at Beginning of Period

Well, that's all there is to it! Where the beauty lies is being able to dissect these sections and gauge the performance, position and lifecycle of the business. And that is what we'll be learning how to do over the following pages. Let's get to it!

Example Cash Flow Statements

It's best to take a look at some example cash flow statements upfront so we know exactly what we are referring to throughout. These are below, but please take on board the next few paragraphs (above the examples) so you have a quick explanation of their source, their similarities and where & why they are different.

Why we are using Two Examples

When it comes to cash flow statements there are two different ways to format the cash flow from operating activities. These two different methods result in the 'direct' cash flow statement and the 'indirect' cash flow statement.

We will leave the deep dive into the differences in these formats till later in this book, as I would like to spend some time explaining the two formats and thus it wouldn't be suitable to go into it right now before we reach the heart of the book.

But the key idea here is that instead of using one example with one format or another, we will be showing two examples here, a direct cash flow statement and an indirect cash flow statement.

Similarities & Differences between the Two Examples

As it was just explained, the direct and indirect cash flow statements present the cash flow from operating activities differently. However, when it comes to presenting the cash flow from financing activities and the cash flow from investing activities there is no difference at all. Specifically, the data and presentation is identical.

It is only the operating activities section that has differences and results in the different statement types.

So when you take a look at the examples you will see the financing and investing sections have literally been 'cut and pasted' between the two examples.

There are also two other small differences between the two examples that must be mentioned.

These differences aren't in the nuts and bolts of the cash flow statements but are instead in the accompanying 'supplemental info' that appears at the bottom of each of the two statements. You will see that the 'cash paid for interest' and 'cash paid for income tax' that appear in the supplemental info of the indirect statement do not appear in the same place as in the direct statement. Within the direct statement these sections (interest & income tax) appear in the operating activities section.

Now, without getting too confusing too early, this particular difference (with tax & interest) is not a specific difference between direct and indirect statements, in general. Rather, where tax and interest appear often comes down to how a particular company chooses to account for these transactions in their particular statements. In other words, you will find this particular difference is company (or transaction) specific rather than being specific to direct and indirect cash flow statements.

If you want to know the exact rules: taxes should appear in operating activities UNLESS the tax cash flows generated are specifically traceable/identified to cash flows that involves financing or investing activities.

As for interest, interest is based on borrowing and lending, which are financing activities, but you will find that the rules that dictate whether something forms part of operating activities cash flows is dependent on whether it is based on "events that enter into the determination of profit or loss", and interest paid and received does in fact help determine profit or loss (and is thus part of operating activities).

Now I will later explain why Amazon Inc. (the source of the indirect cash flow statement example) used supplemental info for taxes and interest, but I thought it would be better to use these line items in, their more usual, operating activities in the direct cash flow statement example (that I generated myself). Just note the conjecture, vague rules & various treatments when it comes to taxes & interest …and hence the final differences between the two example statements.

Source of Examples

Example 1 (Indirect Cash Flow Statement):

As in the previous two titles of this series we will be looking at real-world financial statements. And once again these will be sourced from Amazon Inc. We will be looking at the annual cash flow statements from 2013, that is, from 1st January 2013 to 31st December 2013.

You can find cash flow statements like these from Google Finance or from any listed entity's Investor Relations website. Below, we will be using the 'Consolidated Statement of Cash Flows' from Amazon's 2013 Annual Report that I found at the Amazon.com Investor Relations website. The reason for using this version is that it has more detail than the Google Finance option.

Example 2 (Direct Cash Flow Statement):

Because the Amazon Annual Report uses the indirect method for its cash flow statement, I am unable to source a real-world direct cash flow statement for the company. And after a little searching, I found it quite hard to find a listed entity that presents its cash flow statement (in their annual reports) in the direct method.

Due to this apparent lack of availability, Example 2 will NOT be a real-world cash flow statement.

While I will cut and paste the financing and investing sections (as mentioned earlier), I will be creating a 100% fictional operating activities section. So, please, never rely on this example as being a representation of any actual, real business.

Yes, I will be making up the figures so the cash flow equation holds and that everything looks semi-realistic, but this example is for illustration only and shouldn't be relied upon.

What's more important with this example is that you see some of the common operating activity categories that will appear and that you will be able recognise these when you come across them.

Further, it's important that you should be able to differentiate between the direct and indirect cash flow statements and not be thrown a curveball whenever you come across either.

The Cash Flow Statements

Example 1 (Indirect): Amazon, Inc.

2013

CASH AND CASH EQUIVALENTS, BEGINNING OF PERIOD
    8,084

Operating Activities

Net Income (loss)	274

Adjustments to reconcile net income (loss) to net cash from operating activities:

Depreciation of property and equipment, including internal-use software and website development, and other amortization	3,253
Stock-based compensation	1,134
Other operating expense (income), net	114
Losses (gains) on sales of marketable securities	1
Other expenses (income), net	166
Deferred income taxes	(156)
Excess tax benefits from stock-based Compensation	(78)

Changes in operating assets and liabilities

Inventories	(1,410)
Accounts receivable, net and other	(846)
Accounts payable	1,888
Accrued expenses and other	736
Additions to unearned revenue	2,691

Amortizations of previously unearned revenue (2,292)

Net cash provided by (used in) operating activities   5,475

Investing Activities

Purchases of property and equipment, including
internal-use software and website development   (3,444)
Acquisitions, net of cash acquired, and other   (312)
Sales of marketable securities and other investments   2,306
Purchases of marketable
securities and other investments   (2,826)

Net cash provided by (used in) investing activities   (4,276)

Financing Activities

Excess tax benefits from stock-based compensation   78
Common stock repurchased   0
Proceeds from long-term debt and other   394
Repayments of long-term debt, capital lease,
and finance lease obligations   (1,011)

Net cash provided by (used in) financing activities   (539)

Foreign-currency effect on cash and cash equivalents (86)

**Net increase (decrease) in cash
and cash equivalents**   574

**CASH AND CASH EQUIVALENTS,
END OF PERIOD**   8,658

SUPPLEMENTAL CASH FLOW INFORMATION

Cash paid for interest on long-term debt	97
Cash paid for income taxes (net of refunds)	169
Property and equipment acquired under capital leases	1,867
Property and equipment acquired under build-to-suit leases	877

Example 2 (Direct): Fictional Biz, Inc.

2013

CASH AND CASH EQUIVALENTS, BEGINNING OF PERIOD
     8,084

Operating Activities

Cash receipts from customers	15,175
Cash payments to suppliers	(2,650)
Cash payments to and on behalf of employees	(6,190)
Interest received (paid)	375
Dividends received	650
Cash refunds (payments) of income taxes	(1,885)
Net cash provided by (used in) operating activities	5,475

Investing Activities

Purchases of property and equipment, including internal-use software and website development	(3,444)
Acquisitions, net of cash acquired, and other	(312)
Sales of marketable securities and other investments	2,306
Purchases of marketable securities and other investments	(2,826)
Net cash provided by (used in) investing activities	(4,276)

Financing Activities

Excess tax benefits from stock-based compensation	78
Common stock repurchased	0
Proceeds from long-term debt and other	394
Repayments of long-term debt, capital lease, and finance lease obligations	(1,011)
Net cash provided by (used in) financing activities	(539)
Foreign-currency effect on cash and cash equivalents	(86)
Net increase (decrease) in cash and cash equivalents	574

CASH AND CASH EQUIVALENTS, END OF PERIOD   8,658

SUPPLEMENTAL CASH FLOW INFORMATION

Property and equipment acquired under capital leases	1,867
Property and equipment acquired	

Cash (Flow Statement) is King: The benefits of the cash flow statement

The cash flow statement is probably the most underestimated financial statement of the three majors. When the income statement determines the "bottom line" and it is the balance sheet that determines the equity and net worth of a business, the cash flow statement is far too often overlooked as a real source of accounting information value. But this is definitely not the case! The cash flow statement offers the reader the third angle into the success and position of a business over a period of time. It offers an insight that the income statement and balance sheet are incapable of showing.

And best of all, it complements the other two statements by sort of mixing the strong elements of both the income statement and balance sheet: you can test the performance of a business (like the income statement) by measuring the changes in net assets and cash over a period. You can test the liquidity & solvency (like the balance sheet) of a business by being able to assess its cash generating ability. And these same tests of cash generation abilities (and how the cash is spent) offer a unique measure on how well a company can adapt to future changes in circumstances and taking advantage of new opportunities.

The starkest benefits, as opposed to reading the income statement or balance sheet for value, will now be broken into the following four generalised sub-sections:

You Spend Cash, not Profits

While financial accounting information is based on specific measurement rules, actual business and economic activity (and all the benefits from these) is based on the concept of earning and spending cash. That is, cash and not profit, is what is ultimately earned, spent & enjoyed by business and society.

Being able to assess how well a business can generate cash, which is what the cash flow statement can do, can guide us on how well a company can adapt to the future. Since business activity requires cash to be spent, having good cash generation abilities can dictate whether a business can take advantage of new opportunities (by changing activities through expenditure) when circumstances change.

On a more negative note, it is not a lack of profits that sends a company out of business, it is instead a lack of cash to meet its financial obligations. Thus, being able to measure changes in the levels of cash and being able to assess cash generation abilities going forward is a key cash flow statement benefit.

Speaking as an investor in a particular business (and with outside investors being a primary user group of financial accounting information), it's important to note that dividends (equity investors) and interest (debt investors) are paid in cash, and cash alone. Therefore the cash flow statement benefits investors through helping determine whether dividends and interest will continue to be paid.

Cash & Different Accounting Methods

As was mentioned just before, there are rules that determine how financial accounting data is measured. However these rules do include flexibility and therefore between two different businesses the same exact transaction can be recorded in the income statement and balance sheet in two different ways. This is one of the negative effects of accrual accounting. The cash flow statement removes accrual accounting by only recognising cash transactions and thus the anomalies of different accounting treatments of the same transaction are removed.

The removal of accrual accounting within the cash flow statement has another benefit. It's commonly known that cash transactions are much harder to deliberately manipulate in financial statements if the business' management was doing something fishy. When companies do deliberately manipulate their accounting results, it is normally done with non-cash accounting transactions.

Finally, the removal of accrual and non-cash transactions in the cash flow statement can show the relationship between cash level changes and accounting profit (in the income statement), with all the unique insights and benefits this entails.

Cash & Valuation

You will often find that many financial analysts and experts base their complex valuation models on some sort of 'net present value' of all the expected future cash flows. This reliance on cash flow data for valuation models means that the cash flow statement is perfect to assist in company and project valuation.

Note: Other methods of valuation include using some sort of ratio analysis, if you want to learn a little about ratio analysis, consider checking out of my other books: *"Ratio Analysis Fundamentals: How 17 Financial Ratios Can Allow to Analyse Any Business on the Planet"* (**accofina.com/ratio-analysis-fundamentals.html**)

Cash & Business Success

The way the cash flow statement is broken down between financing, investing and operating cash flows does in fact create a unique view into the business that the income statement and balance sheet can't offer.

Based on the cash flows between these three categories you are able to assess the strategy and lifecycle of any particular business at any point in time. You are able to tell if a company is expanding, contracting and all in between.

And from here you are able to evaluate the success of management decisions. You can see if what they are saying in regards to their strategy is actually matching what is being shown in the cash flow statement.

Further, when management states that the business is 'succeeding' you have immediate reference as to whether this business is a real, cash generating machine or otherwise.

Cash Flows from Financing Activities

Examples of Cash Flows Arising in This Section

1) Cash proceeds from issuing shares or other equity instruments

2) Cash payments to owners to acquire or redeem the entity's shares

3) Cash proceeds from issuing debentures, loans, notes, bonds, mortgages and other short or long-term borrowings

4) Cash repayments of amounts borrowed; and

5) Cash payments by a lessee for the reduction of the outstanding liability relating to a finance lease.

Source: International Accounting Standard 7, Statement of Cash Flows

"Don't forget to also look at the Example Cash Flow Statements at the beginning of this book"

How This Section Feeds into the Cash Flow Equation

Cash at Beginning of Period
+ Cash Flow from Financing Activities

\+ Cash Flow from Investing Activities
\+ Cash Flow from Operating Activities
= Cash at End of Period

What Does This Section Describe

In accounting terminology, the cash flows from financing activity show changes in the long-term liability accounts and the owners' equity accounts.

In more general terminology, this section shows how the business obtained financial resources (from equity and debt investors) or how the business returned financial resources to the same groups. In other words, how the business is raising and returning capital.

Further, you can see what type of capital is being utilised, being debt or equity. The absolute amounts within the data and the categories (similar to those listed above or in the Amazon, Inc. example) describe both how much and what type of capital is raised or returned.

According to the international accounting standards, one of the key benefits of this particular section of the statement is that it is useful at predicting the future claims on business cash flow by the providers of the business' capital. After all, it is the financiers of the business (owners or lenders) who generally receive the benefits of success, as their capital (with a return) is given back to those groups.

What Could the Results Be Telling Us About the Business

Caveat:

This caveat will appear in all applicable analysis sections and is a reminder that this book is meant to be a concise beginners book. As a result, I cannot offer a completely comprehensive description of every possible situation that could be occurring in any possible cash flow statement. The best analysis requires independent inquiry, critical thinking and even maybe a team, and this book is simply too brief to describe every analytical situation under the sun.

However, the cash flow statement does offer unique & apparent insights into a business' lifecycle, strategy and commercial health.

Final Note: None of the insights below are mutually exclusive. There could be mix of any and all of the situations described.

Business Lifecycle:

Starting-Up

A business that shows high cash inflows in the financing sections may indicate that the business is very new or young. Generally, the first activity a business undertakes from its existence is to raise capital that will fund the business in its early stages.

For example, a businessperson may want to start an auto parts manufacturing business and they may approach a bank to get a loan. The loan would show up as a cash inflow in the financing section. The same can be said for a young Silicon Valley entrepreneur when they raise seed capital, however this would normally show us as equity financing and not debt.

Winding-Up

A business showing high cash outflows may be an indicator that the business is winding up or about to close.
When a business is wound up, the last thing it does is pay out all the remaining cash to the owners or lenders of the business. It returns the capital to the financiers as it no longer needs any cash post its existence.

For example, that same auto parts manufacturing businessperson may want to close the business and move into another unrelated line of work. He or she may cease operations, have funds in he bank already and then liquidate all remaining inventory, equipment and property. The complete sum of cash at the end of this process may then pay off the remainder of their bank loan (financing activity outflow) and then return any remaining cash to the shareholders/owners of the business (a similar outflow, but instead an equity outflow).

Business Strategy:

Growth Strategies

Whether raising funds through debt or equity, one of the primary reasons that a business will use external finance (as a strategic measure) is to accelerate growth and take advantage of market opportunities that may be missed if only internal retained earnings were used.

A business has two choices when it wishes to expand (grow), it can use it's own internally generated funds (based on past performance) or it can raise debt/sell equity. Relying on one's own internal funds limits the rate of expansion to the current (or recently experienced) growth rate.

That is, if a business wants to invest $1m in new equipment then building up a cash balance of $1m (to pay for the equipment) is dependant on the current size and growth of the business …and if the business is currently only generating $100k in cash every year then by implication it would take 10-years to have enough cash for the $1m expansion.

However, if that same business made the strategic decision that it wished to grow and expand much faster (possibly taking advantage of a limited time window of opportunity) then it may wish to seek debt finance or equity investment. In this example, getting access to the $1m for the new equipment may only take a couple of weeks or months. This situation is far quicker than the earlier mentioned 10-years and this decision would fundamentally change how the business operates and succeeds (or doesn't) over the following periods.

With this theoretical explanation of strategic financing decisions out of the way you may be want to know what these alternative situations would look like in the cash flow statement.

A business that chooses the strategy of primarily relying on it's own internally generated funds would show few cash inflows in the Financing Activities section. Unless the business has a very fast internal growth rate this choice is generally regarded as a having a lower growth trajectory than the alternative.

As for the alternative: a business that chooses a high growth strategy will generally be trying to access as much external cash as possible to fund their expansion. This will show up as high cash inflows in the Financing Activities section.

Commercial Health:

Rewarding Financiers & Owners

When all is said and done, a major reason why businesses exist is to financially reward the owners (common stockholders) & all financiers (debt & equity, including stockholders) of the business. Not many people start a business and become the initial stockholders unless there will eventually be a payoff.

The same can be said with other investors; not many equity investors will fund a business unless they are going to see a return on these funds. And we can never doubt that debt financiers (such as a bank) are after their financial return. That being said, one could argue that when a business is performing well and succeeding as all those involved had hoped for then surplus funds could be returned to the owners & financiers of the business.

So if you take this on board, when you see large cash outflows in the Financing Activities section of the cash flow statement you may assume that the business is succeeding, that it is stable and that it is generating enough cash on its own that it can now afford to return some of the capital that it had earlier sourced from debt and equity financiers.

These cash outflows may be the payoff from success that all those had hoped for.

Struggling to Generate Cash from Core Operations

If we view the above outflows as a sign of success, we may view high or continued cash inflows in the Financing Activities section as a sign of weaknesses.

Now this may not always be the case, as we just discussed in the lifecycle and strategy section, but for a business to be consistently successful and future-proof itself it must be able to generate a satisfactory level of cash from the core operations of the business. For example, a café must sell enough coffee (consistently) to be successful in the long-term. A sign that a particular café (for example) may not be selling enough coffee is that it keeps seeking out external finance to fund its operations, i.e. the coffee sales are not funding the operations and instead it is the new finance.

This situation may be shown as high or continued cash inflows within this section of the cash flow statement.

Cash Flows from Investing Activities

Examples of Cash Flows Arising in This Section

1) Cash payments to acquire property, plant and equipment, intangibles and other long-term assets. These payments include those relating to capitalised development costs and self-constructed property, plant and equipment

2) Cash receipts from sales of property, plant and equipment, intangibles and other long-term assets

3) Cash payments to acquire equity or debt instruments of other entities and interests in joint ventures (other than payments for those instruments considered to be cash equivalents or those held for dealing or trading purposes)

4) Cash receipts from sales of equity or debt instruments of other entities and interests in joint ventures (other than receipts for those instruments considered to be cash equivalents and those held for dealing or trading purposes)

5) Cash advances and loans made to other parties (other than advances and loans made by a financial institution)

6) Cash receipts from the repayment of advances and loans made to other parties (other than advances and loans of a financial institution)

7) Cash payments for futures contracts, forward contracts, option contracts and swap contracts except when the contracts are held for dealing or trading purposes, or the payments are classified as financing activities, and

8) Cash receipts from futures contracts, forward contracts, option contracts and swap contracts except when the contracts are held for dealing or trading purposes, or the receipts are classified as financing activities

Source: International Accounting Standard 7, Statement of Cash Flows

"Don't forget to also look at the Example Cash Flow Statements at the beginning of this book"

How This Section Feeds into the Cash Flow Equation

Cash at Beginning of Period
+ Cash Flow from Financing Activities
+ Cash Flow from Investing Activities
+ Cash Flow from Operating Activities
= Cash at End of Period

What Does This Section Describe

The Investing Activities describe the cash flows involved in the changes to the long-term asset accounts of the business. In more general terminology, the Investing Activities section shows how a business purchased (outflows) cash generating assets for the business or sold (inflows) the same types of assets. In other words, how the business is making or liquidating long-term business investments.

You may be aware that the accounting definition of an asset is a resource controlled by an entity that will lead to future inflows of cash. Thus being able to measure the purchase (or sale) of these cash inflow generating assets is one of the key benefits derived from this section of the cash flow statement. You can see how a business is deploying its funds in the hope of later earning a higher return on these investments.

Similar to the financing section and as described in the example categories listed above, this section will also describe what type of investment (or disposals) are being made, for example whether these are investments in property, plant & equipment (PPE), purchases of equity instruments in other businesses or even assets being created by making loans. The Investing Section will have all these respective classes listed.

The benefit of this particular section, as described by the international accounting standards, is that it gives the reader of the cash flow statement a broad overview of how the business is making expenditures in the running of the business that will lead to an overall increase in future income and cash flows.

What Could the Results Be Telling Us About the Business

Caveat:

This caveat will appear in all applicable analysis sections and is a reminder that this book is meant to be a concise beginners book. As a result, I cannot offer a completely comprehensive description of every possible situation that could be occurring in any possible cash flow statement. The best analysis requires independent inquiry, critical thinking and even maybe a team, and this book is simply too brief to describe every analytical situation under the sun.

However, the cash flow statement does offer unique & apparent insights into a business' lifecycle, strategy and commercial health.

Final Note: None of the insights below are mutually exclusive. There could be mix of any and all of the situations described.

Business Lifecycle:

Initial Setup

We described earlier that high cash inflows in the financing section were an indicator of a business starting up. Following on from this we can say that high cash outflows within the

Investing Section are the next logical step in the initial setup of a new business.

That is, once a business has raised it's startup finance, the next step a business will undertake to get the business up an running is to invest in an initial set of cash generating assets. This would be shown as high cash outflows within this section of the cash flow statement.

For example, an electronics retailer has initially sourced a bank loan as start up capital. These newly sourced funds may then be deployed to purchase a retail site and maybe then delivery trucks. These asset purchases (the retail site and delivery trucks) are requirements in the initial setup of the business (the business can't operate without these) and would be shown as Investing Section outflows.

Liquidation prior to Wind-Up

At the other end of the business lifecycle and once again linking the ideas described in the financing section, if an Investing Section shows high cash inflows then this may be describing a business that is approaching the end of its life; it may be going through the liquidation stage prior to the final wind-up.

When the management of a particular business has made the certain decision that it wishes to close down and no longer operate then it has the responsibility to remove itself from the commercial landscape and return a final set of funds to the financiers & owners of the business. This would normally involve liquidating all saleable assets, pooling all cash (including from the just mentioned sales) and making a final cash payment to owners and financiers. The process of asset liquidation would be shown within the cash flow statement as high cash inflows in the Investing Section, remembering that this section shows changes in the long-term asset accounts.

For example, that same electronics retailer has now decided to close down. It would now no longer need the retail site or delivery trucks (and would need to return all funds to owners & financiers) and thus it would sell these long-term assets. This would result in high Investing Section inflows.

Business Strategy:

Expansion

A business that shows high cash outflows in the Investing Section can be an indicator that the business is undergoing a period of expansion.

When a business wishes to make the strategic decision to expand and increase the scale of its operations it must invest in assets beyond the normal replenishment of its current asset base. That is, if it wishes to generate income beyond its current level this would require a level of assets (that would generate this higher level of income) greater than what currently stood. This increased level of assets would be shown as high cash outflows in the Investing Section of the cash flow statement.

The example we can use here is one of a bookkeeping service

business that wishes to expand into a new region of the United States. Within its current situation it has a fully equipped commercial office in Seattle and a certain level of property, plant & equipment within the long-term asset accounts would measure this.

But management has made the strategic decision that would like to expand operations (and hopefully grow future income) by moving into the Los Angeles market. It decides to simply replicate its Seattle operations within a second region and thus decides to make an investment in a second fully equipped commercial office.

As the new commercial office and furnishings are purchased this would be shown as high cash outflows in the Investing Section as the property, plant & equipment account is increased.

Contraction

The opposite of what we just talked about can be said in regards to a strategic decision to contract a business.
In that case there would be Investing Section cash inflows as assets were sold to reflect the business decreasing in size.

We won't focus on this situation beyond we was just said (as the explanation is just the reverse of the mentioned expansion section).

Transition in Operations

A more unique situation that could be indicated within this

section is when a business is transitioning its operations. This particular situation may occur when a business has altered it's strategy as is changing the nature of its business, for example changing its geographic footprint of maybe the lines of business it operates within.

If this is the case then certain assets (that were part of the old way of the business was run) may be liquidated, and thus be shown as high cash inflows, and new assets (that will form part of the new way of doing business) may be purchased and thus be shown as high cash outflows.

Depending on how quickly this transition takes place will determine the timeline between when these inflows and outflows take place in a cash flow statement or number of cash flow statements.

Commercial Health:

Expansion as a Result of Success

As was earlier discussed, high cash outflows can be an indicator of business expansion as an entity purchases more and more long-term assets. If we link this idea with the theory that most businesses want (at their very core) to grow and expand consistently over time then we may be able to draw a conclusion that when a business is expanding then it is showing signs of overall success, and strong commercial health, with its core operations.

That is, if a business is achieving its overall objectives,

performing well and selling all the widgets it planned to, then it may be generating enough cash to comfortably fund an expansion and increase the scale of its widget sales operation.

This situation of strong commercial health may be indicated by continued cash outflows in the statement.

Liquidations to Cover Weak Operations

The situation may be the reverse when there are continued inflows within the Investing Section. This situation may be an indicator of weak commercial health.

When it comes down to it, a business would like to be generating its cash from the core operations. Ideally, selling widgets at a profit should be generating enough cash to fund all the activities and actions of the business. Thus, it may be a sign of weakness if a business is relying on liquidating assets (Investing Section cash inflows) to fund its activities.

A business may be in need of quick cash, perhaps to pay off debt or otherwise continue core operating activities, and the only source of funds may be to liquidate assets.

While there is nothing specifically impractical about this strategy, it can definitely be seen as only a short term strategy and could even be very disruptive to future plans.

It is short-term in nature as there are only so many assets you can sell; you can't sell assets forever! And it may be disruptive to future plans as it is the long-term assets that generate future income and if you start 'selling the farm' then a business will be less capable of generating income down the track.

Cash Flows from Operating Activities

Why This Section Has Been Left Till Last

When it comes to cash flow from Operating Activities many regard this at the most important section of the cash flow statement. You may then be wondering why it has been left till last, within this book, of the three main sections.

There are two major reasons why this has been done so:

(1) To account for the chronology of a standard business and how this fits into the business lifecycle that has been described.

(2) The fact that the cash flow from Operating Activities can be presented in two separate, but two equally valid, formats. These two formats create the 'direct' and 'indirect' cash flow statements.

While the International Accounting Standards Board encourages the use of the direct method, you will find that a vast many companies instead use the indirect method. In fact, within my own local jurisdiction (Australia) the accounting regulators require that a reconciliation of Operating Activities cash flows to net income also be provided within a financial report (which is almost, if not, identical to the indirect method) if the direct method is otherwise chosen.

Being able to understand and navigate both the direct

and indirect methods of Operating Activities cash flows really is a required skill if you wish to tackle cash flow statements on an ongoing basis. While they ultimately report the same information (changes in cash flow from operating activities), their presentation is starkly different, and do indeed contain different component pieces of data within.

To the uninitiated, financial statement rookie the 'complication' created by the two different statement formats may have been a little too confusing to introduce earlier in the book. Now that you have covered much of the cash flow statement already and been introduced to complimentary theory, taking on the two different statements is a much easier bridge. Hence, cash flow from Operating Activities has been left till last.

Business Chronology:

Have you noticed as you progress through this book, within the financing & investing activities sections, that the business lifecycle has been following some sort of chronology?

First we talked about a start-up raising finance (financing activities) and then we talked about using this capital to make asset investments that will hopefully generate future income (investing activities). Well operating activities is the next step of this process, we now have everything in place (from financing and investing activities) and it's now time to get down to it and run the actual business.

If you can grasp the above paragraph at this point, then you may already have a clear understanding of what cash flow from Operating Activities is describing within its section. The lifecycle flow and implied understanding (just mentioned) of what this cash flow statement section displays is a core reason why this section is left till last in the book.

Direct & Indirect Cash Flow Statements:

At the beginning of this chapter and also earlier in the book we discussed that there are two different formats for the Operating Activities cash flows. Beyond this earlier introduction, now we will just get down to explaining what makes up the two formats …just don't forget the key idea that the same information (underlying cash flows) are being displayed, only how these are presented is different.

Direct Cash Flow Statement

The direct cash flow statement takes all cash transactions (within the Operating Activities section) and groups them according to major classes, for example 'cash receipts from sales of goods' or 'cash payments to employees'.

You will find that categorising cash transaction according to classes is a very similar formatting option to what is used in (and what you have already read about) the financing and investing cash flow sections. In other words, a direct cash flow statement will look and feel similar between all sections of the cash flow statement.

The International Accounting Standards Board (IASB) encourages businesses to use the direct method on the premise that is better assists the cash flow statement readers in estimating future cash flows, as opposed to the indirect method that may disguise this predictive information.

Indirect Cash Flow Statement

The indirect method presents the same underlying information but takes a different route to get there. What the indirect method does is take net income as a starting figure and then works backwards, by adjusting net income for non-cash accounting transactions, to reach the final cash flow from operating activities.

This method will thus appear not as a section of 'classes of transactions' but instead as a series of non-cash adjustments, from net income to operating activities cash flows. For instance, 'net income' plus 'depreciation/amortisation', plus or minus 'deferred taxes', plus or minus 'changes in working capital', etc.

This method appears more like an arithmetic process as opposed to the classification process within the direct method.

Examples of Cash Flows Arising in This Section

IMPORTANT NOTE: While the direct and indirect methods

look different in presentation, they both capture the same underlying examples of cash flows listed here. That is, the examples listed below are actual Operating Activities cash flows irrespective of how they are presented, direct or indirect.

1) Cash receipts from the sale of goods and the rendering of services

2) Cash receipts from royalties, fees, commissions and other revenue

3) Cash payments to suppliers for goods and services

4) Cash payments to and on behalf of employees

5) Cash receipts and cash payments of an insurance entity for premiums and claims, annuities and other policy benefits

6) Cash payments or refunds of income taxes unless they can be specifically identified with financing and investing activities, and

7) Cash receipts and payments from contracts held for dealing or trading purposes.

Source: International Accounting Standard 7, Statement of Cash Flows

"Don't forget to also look at the Example Cash Flow Statements at the beginning of this book"

How This Section Feeds into the Cash Flow Equation

Cash at Beginning of Period
+ Cash Flow from Financing Activities
+ Cash Flow from Investing Activities
+ Cash Flow from Operating Activities
= Cash at End of Period

What Does This Section Describe

As was implied earlier in the context of the business chronology, the cash flows from Operating Activity provide information on how the cash generates and spends cash in regards to core functions of the business.

If we looked upon Amazon Inc. as an online book retailer (which is a simplification considering the vast array of activities Amazon actually undertakes) then the cash flow from Operating Activities would describe how Amazon spends and makes cash running a book store and selling books, i.e. cash flows from its core *operations* or functions.

The same can be said with any business and any cash flow statement, the Operating Activities are the 'nuts and bolts' of running that particular business. Anything that involves spending or generating cash in the sale of widgets, or whatever, is displayed here.

It was mentioned earlier that many regard the Operating Activities section as the most important section of them all. The emphasis on this section is not misplaced. After all, analysing cash flows within Apple's iPhone selling business or understanding cash flows in The Coca-Cola Company's beverage sales business is critical in justifying the ongoing and very existence of these companies, for example.

Beyond this, even the International Accounting Standard on the Statement of Cash Flows from the IASB (which has been referenced throughout this book) details the important nature of this section.

The Standard describes that the Operating Activities section will give the reader an indication on how well a business can generate cash from it's fundamental operations that will allow it to maintain its ongoing capabilities, repay loans, pay dividends and otherwise make new investments to continue and grow the business without needing new external finance.

Not only does a current cash flow statement display information (the most recent historical Operating Activities performance) but this same information when combined with previous cash flow statements, will also offer the reader useful information in predicting future cash flow generation ability.

Overall, when it comes it Operating Activities cash flows, just remember that these are the cash transactions in managing and *operating* the core business activities.

What Could the Results Be Telling Us About the Business

Caveat:

This caveat will appear in all applicable analysis sections and is a reminder that this book is meant to be a concise beginners book. As a result, I cannot offer a completely comprehensive description of every possible situation that could be occurring in any possible cash flow statement. The best analysis requires independent inquiry, critical thinking and even maybe a team, and this book is simply too brief to describe every analytical situation under the sun.

However, the cash flow statement does offer unique & apparent insights into a business' lifecycle, strategy and commercial health.

Final Note: None of the insights below are mutually exclusive. There could be mix of any and all of the situations described.

Business Lifecycle:

<u>Growth Stages while either (or both) Finding Feet or Within Growing Industry</u>

If you find that a business has increasing levels of Operating Activity cash flows then this may indicate, in regards to the lifecycle, that the business is new and undergoing its initial stages of expansion.

That is, as a new business starts to get its name out into the market, builds its reputation and it progresses through the learning curve of operations you will often find that it can regularly improve on its prior period Operating Activities cash flows. This would result in regular increases in this figure.

Note: this phenomenon doesn't distinguish between positive and negative totals within this section. The key idea is that the total is simply improving over time, irrespective of whether to result leads to overall cash outflows or inflows. In fact, you will often find that the younger the business the more likely that the business will have negative cash flows from Operating Activities. This very young business would just have continually smaller and smaller overall outflows over time.

The second condition mentioned in the sub-heading refers to a growing industry. Within a new or growing industry, you may find that this external environment lifts all boats and leads to increasing cash flows from Operating Activities. By implication, if an industry is growing then you can consider that a business is in the earlier stages of its existence. That is, since the industry is expanding then the businesses would still need to reach and go through the apex of the industry and only then its later stages of decline.

Note: Some industries by their very nature are cyclical and go through repeated peaks and troughs in line with economic conditions or other factors, thus it would be important to investigate this to distinguish between a younger, growing industry (and businesses) indicated by increasing Operating Activities cash flows or simply that a business' results are part of an improvement in a cyclical (but maybe older & declining) industry.

Business Reaches 'Cash-Cow' Status

A (relatively) stable and high level of Operating Activities cash flows is a strong indicator that the business has reached 'cash-cow' status and has everything in place to make it a continually successful business.

So, as we have progressed through the 'Business Lifecycle' sections of this book we have outlined that a business begins its life by raising funds (within the financing activities section) and then it uses these funds to purchase long-term assets (within the investing activities section) and these assets allow the business to maintain the operating capacity of the business and generate income.

From here, and as we just discussed in the previous sub-section, the young business with everything in place then goes through its initial stages of expansion (increasing Operating Activities cash flows).

Now down the track, after all the effort to reach this point, the business is established with well-oiled operations & the industry is some sort of equilibrium.

At this stage of a business' lifecycle you will often find that the there are consistent and relatively stable levels of cash inflows. This is what is termed a 'cash-cow' business; effectively the business owners/farmers can repeatedly draw cash/milk from the fully developed operations of the business/cow.

Business is past its Peak & in Decline

Most products, businesses and industries have a finite lifecycle. Whether it's the horse & cart in the early 20th century or the cassette tape of more recent years, many businesses will naturally run into decline. While a shift in strategy and product transformation can reinvent a business many times over, it is no surprise that most businesses today were not around 100 or 200 years ago or vice versa.

When it comes to the business lifecycle and the point in time that represents a business is now in natural decline you will often find that these particular business find it harder and harder to generate cash flow from Operating Activities.

Thus, this may be evident within the cash flow statement by a repeatedly weaker result in Operating Activity cash flows. Yes, there may still be overall cash inflows within this section but the trend over time will be a deteriorating figure.

Business Strategy:

Firstly, I can think of very few business strategies that wouldn't be aimed at generating the highest level of cash inflow from Operating Activities. This is, after all, the primary purpose of running a business …generating cash from operations!

But there may be a few cases when the structure of cash flows change:

Recent Expansion with Expectation of Growth

This situation would only (hopefully) be temporary, but if a business believes that there are strong opportunities that can be taken advantage of with an increased level of scale then it may have indeed increased its size, with all manner of extra expenses, without yet growing into its new size of operations. Cash inflows from Operating Activities may have suddenly dropped, in this scenario, as a result of the new higher level of operating outflows without (yet) a corresponding increase in the inflows.

For example, a smartphone manufacturer may believe that with a new factory & more factory staff that it may be able to reduce it's unit costs, which may then lead to new contracts with leading smartphone brands while also taking advantage of the growing smartphone market. The new factory's operating expenses (electricity, maintenance, salaries, etc.) will be incurred from day zero but the planned new contracts & market growth and resulting customer inflows may not show up for a year or two. Operating Activities outflows would suddenly increase (at day zero) and not yet have the corresponding inflows.

Acquisitions or Divestments

Whether the relative level of inflows versus outflows changes in this case is dependant on the success of this strategy, but if a business undertakes an acquisition of another business then you will most likely see an increase level of aggregate cash flows. That is the absolute value of these cash flows will increase due to the fact that there is a whole new business within this entity's financial statements.

The reverse is true if a business performs a divestment and sells one of its business units. There is one less entire business within the new cash flow statement.

Change in Business Structure, Organisation or Product Offerings

If there is a fundamental change in how the core business of an entity will be run then there may temporarily be erratic changes in Operating Activities cash flows.

You'll notice cash flows can indeed become predictable when there is little change in the overall running of a business. But when a business makes a strategic decision to change the way it will operate by perhaps changing the organisational structure, the objectives of the business or maybe the products it offers (that is, the core operations of the business) then these changes will become apparent in the cash flow statement.

Until the changes are complete and the core operations of the business become predictable again then there may be transitional changes in the inflows and outflow of Operating Activities.

Commercial Health:

Achieving Business Goals & Performing Well

If a business can achieve consistently high levels of Operating Activities cash flows then there may be few better indicators that a business is performing well and achieving its overall business goals.

Everything that has been presented in this book, in a way, leads to this argument.

The idea that a business starts up & sets up facilities, chooses & finds the best business strategy and releases products that have strong demand all in the hope that it can become successful in its core business operations.

A brilliant indicator of this 'success' is having strong (and ideally growing) inflows within the Operating Activities section of the cash flow statement. It is a black and white indicator that isn't always available from the income statement and balance sheet, alone.

Beyond this, having strong inflows places any business in the best position for long-term success. After all, if there is any possible change that could impact the business in the future what better way to face it and adjust accordingly by drawing on the 'rivers of gold' that the business' operations are providing.

There is only so many times you can tap banks and investors on the shoulder for more money in the future (financing activities) and there are only so many assets you can sell to raise cash for long-term planning adjustments (from the investing activities section). The cash from operating activities is a far deeper well for future resource planning.

What's more (and as was briefly mentioned earlier in the

book), if you do want to repeatedly seek external finance from lenders or equity participants, the best reassurance these financiers can have that they will get their return is that the business is generating consistently strong cash flows from Operating Activities. If you can generate cash consistently then you can pay the financiers interest and dividends consistently.

Not Achieving Business Goals & Performing Poorly

If you can picture the mirror image of what was just described in the previous section then you will already know where I am going in this section…

If a business has Operating Activities outflows or otherwise deteriorating cash flows then this may mean the business is failing to achieve its business goals and is performing badly.

The financing and investing activities sections are used as a foundation to allow success in the Operating Activities section. If you are weak in the latter section then you can't indefinitely rely on the former sections to prop you up.

In regards to outside the cash flow statement, no amount of accounting 'trickery', past results or appearance of strong balance sheets or income statements can protect a business in the long-term if it can't generate sufficient cash from its core operations.

I don't know what else I can say beyond what has been just said and was mentioned in the mirrored previous section, it is never a good sign when a business has weak or weakening results in the Operating Activities section of the cash flow statement.

Final note: Is a series of poor results the death knell for any business at any point in time? The short answer is no. But it is indeed almost always an indicator that something isn't working out as planned or earlier envisaged AND that eventually something is going to have to change within the business to reverse these weak results.

Specific Accounting Issues that may be presented in Cash Flow Statements

Okay, we are now at a point where we have covered all the fundamental lessons from a standard cash flow statement.

However, when you step out of this 'basics' book and start looking at your own 'real-world' cash flow statements then you may encounter a few issues that seem a little more confusing or at least just out of place as to what we have covered till this point.

These issues are based around accounting practices, disclosures and how cash flow statements preparers (normally accountants) deal with the application of their standardised rules to the less standardised variety found in every single different organisation globally.

We are now going to cover a few of these common issues and explain what they represent or least the logic that leads to their appearance in many cash flow statements.

FX Translation Issues

There are two issues when it comes to businesses that deal in currencies other than their main currency.

Note: The currency a business uses in its financial statements is termed the 'presentation currency'.

Transactions occurring in a Foreign Currency:

Things get a bit messy when business has transactions denominated in a foreign currency. This is because of the fact that for 24-hours a day, 5-days a week exchange rates behind these transactions are bouncing all over the place.

How then do cash flow statements account for these oddities? Take an example business that has 1,000,000 transactions during 2016 in Euros when its presentation currency is the US Dollar. How can we interpret and understand the underlying accounting in the 2016 cash flow statement?

Firstly, the businesses will 'translate' the Euro transactions into their USD presentation currency using an exchange rate so all transactions appear as though they are in USD.

But what EUR/USD exchange rate do we use? We are not allowed to just use the exchange rate that prevails at reporting date.

According to financial accounting rules ideally we want to use the exact exchange rate that corresponds with the exact date the transactions took place. But even if we just used daily exchange rates, that means we would have to apply 365 different exchange rates to the 1,000,000 transactions that occurred over the year (depending on what day each of the transactions occurred).

The allowed solution is that you use a weighted average exchange rate for the whole year and apply that one (weighted average) rate to the whole 1,000,000 transactions.

For example if 900,000 transactions occurred on the 1st January (first day of the year) and the remaining 100,000 transactions occurred on the 31st December (last day of the year) then you would find the exchange rates for the 1st January ($0.91) and 31st December ($0.97) and then apply weights of 0.9 (900,000 transactions) and 0.1 (100,000 transactions) to these hypothetical rates to achieve an overall weighted average. Or $0.91 x 0.9 + $0.97 x 0.1 = $0.916 Now all 1,000,000 of the 2016 Euro transactions are translated at a rate $0.916 for the 2016 cash flow statement calculations.

Cash Balances held in a Foreign Currency:

Now we look at businesses that have cash balances denominated in a foreign currency.

Firstly, a change in value of these foreign balances due to changes in exchange rates is NOT a cash flow. No cash has left or come into the organisation. Only the value of the foreign balance has changed and only in respect to the presentation currency. So you will never find these types of changes appearing in operating, investing or financing activities sections.

However, we do have to account for these value changes and disclose them in the cash flow statement. Why? Because if we have a change in value of foreign cash balances then somehow we need to reconcile all our cash flow statement data to the beginning and ending cash balances.

For example, ABC Company has USD $1,000 and EUR $1,000 in bank accounts on the 1st January. Thus our beginning cash balance (assuming at $0.90 USD/EUR exchange rate) would be USD $2,111 (1000 + (1000 / 0.9)).

And now we move to 31st December and the USD/EUR exchange rate is now $0.95. Assuming the balances are the same our ending cash balance is $2053 (1000 + (1000 / 0.95)). If we then plug in all our actual cash flows for the year into operating, investing & financing then our cash flow equation (which I have presented a number of times) will not balance. It will be out by $58 ($2,111 - $2053).

Equations not balancing are the nightmare of all accountants! So what do we do? According to financial accounting rules we need to disclose a separate line item on the cash flow statement that reports this FX value change ($58). By including this new line item we can reconcile beginning to ending cash balances and also make the cash flow equation balance.

Note: this new line item must be separate from the operating, investing and financing sections. That is, it is never fed into one of these sections and will normally sit separately at the bottom of the statement (see the Example Cash Flow Statements towards the beginning of the book).

Significant Non-Cash Disclosures

One of the points behind analysing the investing and financing activities sections of any cash flow statement is that it gives the reader an insight into the asset (investing) and capital (financing) structure of the business.

But this insight can be obscured when 'significant' (large and material) transactions occur in the asset or capital structure when no actual cash changes hand.

For example, take a small to medium business that signs up to a number of leases that will provide the use of assets for the business. A business my get an equipment lease from a bank and receive 150 new notebook computers. No cash may have yet changed hand between the bank and business (the first lease payment may occur in 18-months) or between the business and notebook supplier (the bank may have handed over funds directly to the supplier bypassing the business).

So here we have a dramatic expansion in the business' asset base (the notebooks) that could lead to future income and the business has raised external finance (changed the capital structure) that must be paid back down the track, the finance lease. Yet nothing has appeared in the cash flow statement! It kind of defeats many of the analytical benefits I have been harping on about throughout this book.

There is a solution to this problem, but it may not appear directly within the cash flow statement.

The financial accounting standard setters have made it a requirement that if there are any significant non-cash transactions that would otherwise be presented in the investing or financing sections, then these transactions must be disclosed within the overall, complete financial report. In other words, you will find these transactions specified in the 'Notes to the Financial Statements'.

The Notes to the Financial Statements are the pages of detail that come after the main financial statements within the overall financial report of a business. That is, the main financial statements take up 3 to 5 pages at the beginning of the financial report and then after these statements you will find about 60 pages of 'Notes' that provide more detail into the earlier financial statements, all disclosures as well as outlining all the accounting policies. You will find these 'Significant Non-Cash Disclosures' here in these Notes.

Interest & Dividends

This was spoken about earlier in the book when we were discussing the Example cash flow statements. But now we return to the topics of interest & dividends to discuss what the formal rules are according to the IASB & IFRS.

The bad news:

Even the formal IFRS standards aren't clear as to which section interest and dividends should appear.

You will find that different organisations will place these items in either operating, investing or financing sections. So you will need to keep an eye out for this and be aware when you compare statements from two or more different organisations.

According to the rules, these things are clear:

You keep interest and dividends separate in your reporting, you don't combine them as one line item.

Secondly, once a section of the cash flow statement is chosen then the business needs to remain consistent from period to period. That is, if interest is going to appear in the operating section in 2016 then it shouldn't appear (for example) in the financing section in 2017. The classification should remain consistent over time.

This is what is not clear and where there is no consensus:

Interest (cash flows both ways) & dividends received may be considered an operating activity because these flows feed into the determination of profit & loss (as was mentioned when we discussed this earlier).

Dividends paid (not received) do NOT feed into profit and loss and thus you can't make the same argument about them appearing in the operating section. But on the other hand, some cash flow statement readers may want to determine a business' ability to pay dividends from core operations and then in this case you would put in it the operating activities section.

But interest & dividends (inflows & outflows) may also be a financing activity as they involve cash flows in regards to obtaining external financial resources and it involves the capital structure of a business.

Further, interest & dividends (inflows & outflows) may also even be an investing activity as the cash flows may be tied to the return on investment of particular long-term assets.

Confusing? Yes. And why this section is included in the book.

Just remember that the choice will often be company or transaction specific, interest & dividends will always be presented separately and that once a choice is made then the business should remain consistent from period to period and keep the cash flows in the same section.

Taxes

Okay, now we are up to our final tricky section, I hope you are still hanging in there with me.

When it comes to tax cash flows it is another situation where there is no definitive rule about which section the cash flow should appear in. Whether they appear in operating, investing or financing is transaction or accounting period specific.

The general rule is that tax cash flows should appear in operating activities. This feeds back into the idea that tax is involved in the calculation of profit & loss.

But there is an exception. If a specific tax cash flow can be traced to a specific transaction that appears in the investing or financing sections and the transaction and resulting tax cash flow occur in a comparable accounting period, then you may find this tax cash flow appears in the investing or financing section whichever the case may be.

Further, if a business finds that the tax cash flows are a mishmash of operating, investing & financing flows and placing them in a single section would appear inappropriate then a single separate tax flow figure may be disclosed separately from all sections in a new line item. This is what may be the case with the Example Amazon Inc. statement that appears towards the beginning of this book (and as I mentioned I would refer to later).

Final Thoughts

Well that wraps up the book and also wraps up this Financial Statement Basics series! Thanks for your time and interest. As for final thoughts on this book, I hope that you can keep it both as a reference for the future while also it being only your first step in your cash flow statement analysis journey.

If you want to learn more theory then almost any accounting textbook you could find will provide a chapter or two on the cash flow statement …and often in more detail than this concise 35-page book.

Further, if you want to go to the source of financial accounting rules then you could always check out 'International Accounting Standard (IAS) 7: Cash Flow Statements'. The International Accounting Standards Board (IASB) is the organisation that has released IAS 7.

The best way to learn about most fields of interest is to put theory into practice. Thus I hope you go, get out there and get a hold of as many real-world cash flow statements that you can handle. Use the lessons in this book as a basis but be prepared to adjust your knowledge for all the intricacies that you will face.

And don't be frightened when you first venture out and various cash flow statements all look a little different! Don't forget about the differences between direct and indirect statements and keep in mind the slightly odd different accounting treatments of things like interest, tax, etc.

You will soon find out that more cash flow statements you look at the easier the analysis process will become. Very quickly you will be able to tell new stories about businesses (from the cash flow statement) that were previously obscured from you. Very quickly you'll realise that this whole process isn't as difficult as first imagined!

Thanks again for your time with this book, I sincerely hope you got more practical value in return than the investment of time & money in reading & acquiring the title

Best wishes,

Axel Tracy

Extras

Book Excerpt

The book you just read hopefully helped you get up to speed with the financial statements. And I'm assuming one of the reasons you wanted to do this was so that you could conduct some sort of financial statement analysis for your own business or any other investment. Well you may be interested in another type of financial statement analysis, *ratio analysis*.

Ratio analysis uses financial statement data to calculate financial ratios that in turn can be used to assess the performance, position and general status of any business.

As was mentioned in Cash Flow Statement Basics, my most successful book to date has been *"Ratio Analysis Fundamentals: How 17 Financial Ratios Can Allow You To Analyse Any Business on the Planet"*.

Well, I would like to offer you an excerpt from this title both to say thanks for reading the book you just read and to encourage you to possibly buy 'Ratio Analysis Fundamentals' as well.

You will find the book excerpt below (this section is about the 'Return on Assets') and you can find out more info and how to

buy Ratio Analysis Fundamentals at:
accofina.com/ratio-analysis-fundamentals.html

Please enjoy the following excerpt!

RETURN ON ASSETS

Along with the return on equity, the Return on Assets is one of the most fundamental measures of the success of a business. It takes pre-tax profit, adds back the interest expense and uses the result in a ratio against the assets of the business. What it is telling us is the return generated by the assets of the business for those who funded the assets, these being the stockholders (pre tax profit) and creditors (interest expense). It is measured as a percentage of the average level of assets over the period.

Why is so much emphasis placed on the Return on Assets? This is because it is a simple indicator to calculate while giving great insight into the success of management to those who fund, or own, the business but are outside of management. After all, the money shareholders or creditors invest in the business is allocated by management in the purchase on income generating assets. That is, the normal lifecycle of a business is that (a) it raises funds (b) invests in assets (c) makes a return on those assets (d) gives back the returns to those who funded the assets. Thus, you want to know (as a creditor, investor or manager) that the income-generating aspect of the business is generating a decent return. If asset allocation decisions are good and the assets are run well, then the

Return on Asset figure will also be strong.

The Formula:

Return on Assets =
(Income Before Tax + Interest Expense) / ((Assets at Start of Period + Assets at End of Period) / 2)

Example from given Financial Statements:

Return on Assets
= ($1,955,550 + $85,000) / (($12,326,000 + $12,893,940) / 2)
= 16.18%

Where do we find the information for this ratio?

Income Before Tax: In the Income Statement (Profit & Loss Statement)
Interest Expense: In the Income Statement (Profit & Loss Statement)
Assets at Start of Period: In the previous Balance Sheet
Assets at End of Period: In the current Balance Sheet

What the result means:

As mentioned, the result is a percentage. So if you have a Return on Assets of 18% this means for every dollar of assets in the business, 18% (or 18 cents) of that is available as a return for those who fund the business.

What it means if the Return on Assets changes:

So what does an increasing Return on Assets mean? Generally it means your profitability has increased in relation to your level of assets.

The reasons behind this incorporate all the business decisions within a period. It could be a reduction in expenses or increase in revenue, all while holding relative assets constant. And further behind these, it essentially means that management is improving their performance. Their decisions are resulting in getting "more for less" or at least more returns for the same inputs.

Another reason behind an increasing Return on Assets is that the assets are being consumed while there isn't the capital spending to maintain (or replenish) their levels. This situation is trickier to assess because while the ratio is improving, no business should completely let their income generating assets diminish without replacing them. It again might be important to look at other information to determine which of the above two situations is occurring.

Let's look at the previous section's latter situation first when we analyze the reverse situation, and the Return on Assets is declining. This can occur when assets have suddenly increased and the profitability is yet to do the same. This can often be the case when large asset investments have a lag time before the profitability ends up in the books. Again, look into the strategy of the business to determine if this is the case.

On a more negative note, a declining Return on Assets can simply mean that the assets aren't performing as they once did, or those new large asset investments are never showing up as profitability in the books.

This once again boils down to management performance. Whether it's competitive pressure, bad strategy or being unable to counter an economic downturn, the nature of the ratio means that most performance inputs are being incorporated (income before tax from the profit and loss statement and asset levels from the balance sheet) and these are management decisions.

Drawbacks of the Return on Assets Ratio:

The Return on Assets does have its drawbacks. Firstly, like many other ratios, it's difficult to make comparisons between businesses that are in different industries and this can severely limit the investment benefits unless you are certain you will invest in a particular industry. Take a new Silicon Valley start-up as an example, they wouldn't spend as much on assets as a mining business. Most of the start-up's early costs would be wage and marketing expenses until it generated some of its own intellectual property assets, while a mining company without enormous levels of fixed assets would be breaking the norm. So when comparing Vale or BHP Billiton to Twitter or Facebook, whose Return on Assets (ROA) figure is better?

As mentioned earlier, while an increasing Return on Assets figure is generally very positive, businesses can reduce their assets to very low levels and increase this ratio. Keeping a very low asset base isn't always something that should be encouraged.

Finally, the most common way assets are reduced is through depreciation and amortization (amortization is depreciation for intangible assets). And depreciation policy is a management choice and there are different, perfectly acceptable (and legal) options when it comes to choosing how to depreciate assets. Therefore choice of depreciation policy can impact the Return on Assets. For example two companies may be identical in all respects, but one uses straight-line depreciation and other uses reducing-balance depreciation. The one using reducing-balance depreciation would have a higher ROA earlier on throughout the life of the asset, because its assets levels are reduced faster early in the life of the asset with the reducing-balance method.

Free (and One Paid) Accounting Resources

IFRS & IASB (http://www.ifrs.org) The International Accounting Standards Board and International Financial Reporting Standards Foundation have a joint website. Often these Standards and rule-setting board are referred to in this book, so why not go directly to the source yourself. Here you will find a wealth of information regarding financial accounting. It may seem a little complex or overbearing early on, but once you become more familiar with accounting jargon, then this source is the top of the pyramid.

FASB (http://www.fasb.org) The Financial Accounting Standards Board is the US equivalent of the IASB. The FASB are the rule-setters in an American context and create the generally accepted accounting principles, or more commonly referred to as GAAP.

Introduction to Financial Accounting: Coursera (https://www.coursera.org/learn/wharton-accounting) If you want a quick, clear and kind of funny series of video lectures and tasks that can get you up to speed with all the fundamentals of bookkeeping and accounting then you may want to check this Coursera course. It's free, published by the Wharton School and has numerous sessions (including archived sessions). It covers accounting fundamentals told through the story of financial statements and ratio analysis.

Financial Markets: Coursera (https://www.coursera.org/learn/financial-markets)

This Coursera course is your opportunity to be taught by an Economics Nobel Prize winning professor, the famous Robert Shiller from Yale University. This Coursera version is a condensed version of a Yale course, with all the most important bits of financial institutions, markets, history of financial thought and all in between. The quality of the guest speakers you are offered is testament to this course being of the best in the world that is available in a MOOC.

SEC's EDGAR (http://www.sec.gov/edgar.shtml) The EDGAR website, which is produced by the US Securities & Exchange Commission, has an immense amount of financial and company data from US businesses. Specifically, companies are required to submit financial reports, annual reports, etc. to the SEC and the EDGAR website allows any visitor to access and download any of these submitted reports. In other words, you will be able to access the financial statements of any US listed business any time you want.

Google Finance (https://www.google.com/finance) Google's finance website is still probably one of the individual investor's best free sources of financial data and information on the web. It contains a world-class stock screener, has financial statement information for more companies than you can poke a stick at as well as strong charting capabilities. Seriously, I'm glad Google makes so much money with AdWords so they can offer cool sites like this one for free (…and create driverless cars!)

Accounting [9th Edition]: Horngren, Harrison & Oliver

[Paid] (http://www.amazon.com/Accounting-9th-Charles-T-Horngren/dp/0132569051/)

This link takes you to the Amazon Product Page of a recent edition of the accounting book that I used in my first-year accounting studies at university. At UTS we used this book in two semesters of accounting study for both introductory financial and management accounting. If you can get through this dense book (it's a full blown textbook) then you'll be very proficient with accounting overall. I'm pretty sure the link takes you to the US Edition, as I couldn't find my original Australian edition, so it may have wider localised appeal.

Free accofina.com Resources

'accofina' is the business behind this book and within its website, accofina.com, you will find a number of free resources available for download or for use on-site:

Accounting Introduction PDF mini-book
(http://accofina.com/accounting-foundations.html)
"Accounting: Foundation Inputs & Outputs" is a 15-page PDF mini-book which is available for download. It offers some of the basic accounting theory into the inputs and outputs of a financial accounting system. The outputs are the three main financial statements and the inputs being the theory behind accounting data entry, including debit and credit rules.

Ratio Analysis Spreadsheet
(http://www.accofina.com/ratio-analysis-excel.html)
You will find 17 of the most common financial ratios have been put into a MS Excel Spreadsheet which both calculates the ratios as well as offering the formulae behind them.

Capital Budgeting Spreadsheet
(http://accofina.com/capital-budgeting-excel.html) If you wish to assess the value of planned large projects and capital expenditures then you may benefit from capital budgeting tools. You can access a spreadsheet that does a lot of number crunching and provides NPVs, pro forma income statements as well as other information just by inputting some key project data.

Time Value of Money Spreadsheet
(http://accofina.com/time-value-money-excel.html)
The Time Value of Money is one of the most important concepts in finance. This available spreadsheet calculates some of the primary time value of money concepts such as future values, present values and annuities. All formulae are also provided within.

Cash Flow Forecast Spreadsheet
(http://accofina.com/cash-flow-forecast-excel.html)
The final spreadsheet offered by accofina is a 2-year monthly cash flow forecast to assist in planning and control. It provides a strong overview of 24-months and also calculates running balances, aggregate totals and overdraft interest.

Online Finance Calculators (accofina.com) has 25 on-site finance calculators available for use for free. Many calculators involve the financial statements and there are other finance, business and investment calculators. They are simple JavaScript calculators where you simply enter the financial data and the calculator displays the result. A brief guidance explanation is also offered with all calculators.

More Books and Other accofina Products

More Books:

1) Ratio Analysis Fundamentals

http://accofina.com/ratio-analysis-fundamentals.html

2) Corporate Finance Fundamentals

http://accofina.com/corporate-finance-fundamentals.html

3) 331 Great Quotes for Entrepreneurs

http://accofina.com/331-great-quotes-entrepreneurs.html

4) Balance Sheet Basics (Book 1 of Financial Statement Basics)

http://accofina.com/balance-sheet-basics.html

5) Income Statement Basics (Book 2 of Financial Statement Basics)

http://accofina.com/income-statement-basics.html

6) Cash Flow Statement Basics (Book 3 of Financial Statement Basics)

http://accofina.com/cash-flow-statement-basics.html

Online Courses and Tutorials:

1) Financial Statement Fundamentals (Udemy Course)

http://accofina.com/financial-statement-fundamentals.html

2) Udemy Instructor Page
www.udemy.com/u/axeltracy/

3) YouTube
www.youtube.com/accofina

iOS Apps:

1) Ratio Analysis & Management Accounting Calculators
http://accofina.com/management-accounting-ratio-analysis-app.html

2) Ratio Analysis & Management Accounting Calculators 'Lite'
http://accofina.com/lite-management-accounting-ratio-analysis-app.html

3) Profitable Pricing
http://accofina.com/profitable-pricing-app.html

accofina Contact Details and Review Request

You can contact me, Axel Tracy, at accofina anytime and for any reason at any of these contact points. Tell me if you enjoyed the book, or if you could suggest anything for a 2nd edition.

Email: **axel@accofina.com**

Facebook: **facebook.com/accofinaDotCom**

Twitter: **@accofina**

Google+: **https://plus.google.com/+accofina**

Amazon Review Request:

Also, it would be great to get an Amazon Review from you if you enjoyed, and got value, from this book.

Positive Amazon Reviews are worth their weight gold in the Amazon World and could possibly propel my little business, accofina, beyond its wildest expectations.

If you did get a positive experience from this book, it would be deeply appreciated if you could spare a couple of minutes to Rate the Book (on its Amazon product page) and maybe leave a positive Comment. Thanks again.

Made in the USA
Las Vegas, NV
08 December 2021